ISBN 978-1-66782-279-2

Contents

Lincoln, METCO and the MCC

In September of 1966, Lincoln was one of the seven towns that first participated in METCO (Metropolitan Council for Educational Opportunity), a school integration program that enrolls Boston students in grades K-10 in participating suburban public schools to reduce racial isolation. Although transportation and other operational expenses are funded by the Commonwealth of Massachusetts, the town's METCO Coordinating Committee or MCC (also known as the Friends of Lincoln METCO) raised money each year to subsidize Lincoln summer camp scholarships; additional transportation for events sponsored by the PTO, MCC, and the town; and supplies for enrichment workshops that would afford Boston-resident and Lincoln-resident students the opportunity to build community outside of the classroom.

In 2017, Joanna Schmergel became the fundraising chair of the Lincoln MCC. She hit upon the idea of soliciting donations of furniture, antiques, artwork and other estate items, then selling them and using the proceeds to create an endowment for the MCC that would fund summer camp for LincolnMETCO students in perpetuity. The committee and Marika Hamilton, the Lincoln METCO Director and AIDE Coordinator, stayed connected on the project and to ensure that MCC's support was aligned with the enrichment needs of the program.

This is not just a fundraising story or a book about how to sell estate items. This is a visual testimonial about how a small group of people, with no expertise in fundraising or estate sales, organized and inspired the Lincoln community and supporters across the greater Boston area to raise over $122,000 in under four years — a journey that took place amidst a global pandemic and a dark time in our country. We learned through a variety of experiences and now we're passing on our acquired knowledge to show that anyone can do this on any scale to raise any amount of money.

This is a success story about how the MCC and everyone else involved — the Lincoln School, students, caregivers, donors, buyers, local organizations, and many citizens of our beautiful Commonwealth — practiced the art of collaboration around a common purpose and brought the MCC vision to life.

We wrote this book for other "Friends of METCO" groups across Massachusetts, in the hope that sharing our experiences supports your fundraising endeavors. We hope that by reaching you, we can start the process of forming relationships across all 33 communities and support all of our students in having culturally enriching experiences.

Dedication

This book is dedicated to Dr. Kizzmekia "Kizzy" Corbett, a viral immunologist. Her work at the National Institute of Allergy and Infectious Diseases' Vaccine Research Center was part of groundbreaking research that directly led to development of the Moderna COVID-19 vaccine. Her work will save millions of lives and also get MCC estate sales up and running again!

Lincoln MCC's mission and vision

The Lincoln MCC supports building a strong, antiracist community in which students and families with different life experiences feel a deep sense of inclusion and belonging and recognize, accept, and celebrate each other's differences. We also support the METCO program by activating caregivers to help attain its goals and priorities. We will achieve this by:

- Creating opportunities for Lincoln resident and Boston resident students and caregivers to build authentic and lasting relationships and an equitable exchange of welcoming experiences in both Boston and Lincoln (e.g., opportunities for social connection, after school programming for children, summer camp)

- Supporting the school and community in its antiracism, inclusion, diversity and equity work (e.g., district National Coalition Building Institute training, caregiver education)

- Advocating and supporting the METCO program at the state and local levels

- Organizing funding and volunteers in support of the METCO team with their work

- Advocating for conditions that will promote a truly integrated public school environment (an inclusive curriculum, a vision for integration, etc.)

Downsize for Diversity: how it all started

Downsize for Diversity began with a simple act when we accepted a generous donation of 60 Franklin Mint porcelain dolls (many of them broken) and started to sell them to collectors through an eBay store.

After a few weeks of watching and learning about the online doll resale market, we decided that we could earn more money by selling American Girl dolls. A community call for gently loved American Girl dolls and accessories yielded dozens of donations, and we found ourselves designing gift baskets that we ultimately sold locally, priced at just $58 each to sell the most dolls in the shortest period of time.

Community members got wind of our successful doll resale endeavor and suddenly started offering us other donated collectibles and home furnishings—artwork, china, rugs, antiques. This catapulted us into the estate sale world. Over the course of four years, we collected items from 252 different donors across 33 Massachusetts towns, resulting in 655 bulk and individual sales. Additionally, we hosted three two-day estate sales events during this time, which not only allowed us to raise critical funds for our organization, but also helped us educate people about the METCO program and the MCC's mission.

COVID-19 forced us to suspend estate sale operations. Nevertheless, just three weeks before the four-year goal line, we rocketed past our $100,000 goal to achieve net sales of over $122,000. This money is now in an investment fund that is governed by clear spending guidelines and parameters.

MCC member Hope White (left) and Joanna Schmergel, MCC's fundraising director during the Downsize for Diversity project.

MCC Secretary Becky Bermont and her daughter.

The MCC's Gina Halstead and Joanna Schmergel in front of "Big Bertha," Joanna's pickup truck that transported dozens of donated pieces.

Our first sales foray: naked porcelain dolls

25% of our first donation of porcelain dolls came to us broken. However, we discovered that eBay has a market for everything—even for doll collectors who need doll parts and clothing! We sold and shipped both intact and broken dolls as part of our Broken Porcelain Hearts Collection.

This Marilyn Monroe porcelain doll wears an authentication number just below her tan line.

Lincoln MCC's doll shop opens!

American Girl dolls: a–tisket, a–tasket, lots of 'em in baskets

"When Joanna is in the room, no idea is too big, nor is there a detail too small. She takes ideas, applies her full heart and enthusiasm and makes magic happen. That's what happened with the American Girl Doll idea. She recognized a market for American Girl doll resale, and the donations (dolls, clothes, accessories, baskets) came pouring in. Then the buyers followed with equal enthusiasm!"

— Pilar Doughty,
former MCC President

There was lots of enthusiasm to donate, but that meant that some of the dolls arrived a little more than "gently loved." We began taking the dolls that needed serious repairs to the old American Girl Doll shop in Natick, Mass., for rehab. We even found four dolls at the swap table at the Lincoln transfer station, where people bring their trash and recycling. We sent them away and they came back in brand-new condition. But this was expensive.

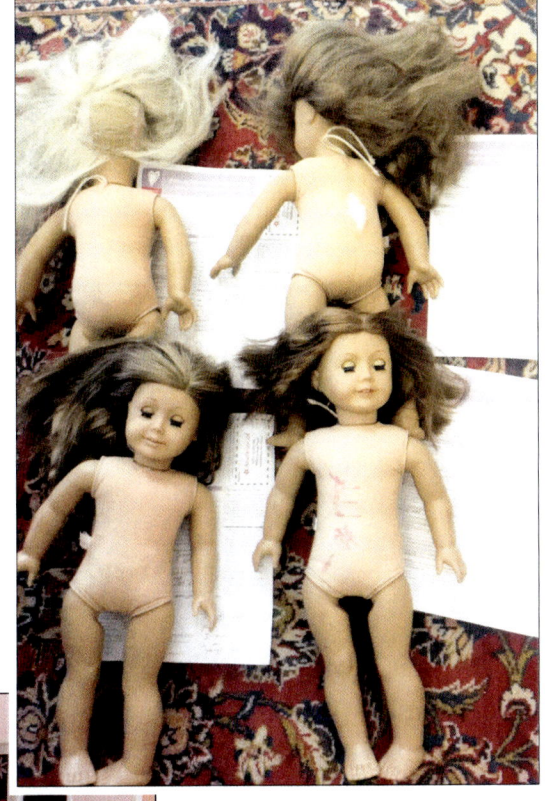

Paging "Doctor" Howell...

We needed a doll doctor, and luckily, Joanna met Darcy Howell, a former American Girl Doll employee and Brandeis student studying early childhood education, when Darcy came to buy American Girl items. We quickly snapped her up onto our team! Darcy saved us as much as $100 per doll in rehab costs at the American Girl "Doll Hospital" by replacing wigs and heads, tightening loose limbs, and re-stuffing torn dolls.

Needs Both Legs Tightened

Needs All 4 Limbs Tightened

A lot of work went into getting the dolls and donated items into sellable doll baskets. We learned that baking soda and water can remove most stains from the plastic parts of the dolls. Use nail polish remover only as a last resort, as it removes the painted parts of the doll's skin like the eyebrows, and then you have to replace the entire head!

11

American Girl doll sales lead to the next MCC venture...

the Social Entrepreneurship Program

During the summer of 2019, Marika Hamilton became the Lincoln School's METCO Director and AIDE Coordinator. She literally jumped right into working with MCC by enthusiastically hopping in the front seat of Joanna's Dodge Ram, a.k.a. Big Bertha, for the Fourth of July parade in Lincoln to support the work and messaging around diversity, equity, and inclusion.

That day was the start of something magical. Joanna and Marika (both Simmons College alumnae) met at Joanna's home and brainstormed some ideas. One of those ideas was realization that combining the efforts of students and the MCC would have a greater impact than the sum of their parts. Marika thought that it would be powerful to have Boston students involved in their own cause, and thus the Social Entrepreneurship Program was born.

Students from Boston and Lincoln took up crafts and sewing, creating fleece hats and baskets for the American Girl dolls. Although they knew their work would be American Girl Doll baskets to be sold at the MCC estate sale, they also took this opportunity to learn about entrepreneurship. They learned about topics such as the four P's of marketing (Product, Price, Promotion, Place), collecting data through surveys, target markets, profit, debt, revenue, and supply and demand. Ultimately, the students designed and launched companies around their new passion. One business venture was a motivational speaking/mentoring program called YES! (Youth Empowerment Speakers).

As plans for the Social Entrepreneurship Program progressed, there was also a shift taking place in the country around race and racism. The program offered a golden opportunity to have students reflect on and engage in deeper learning that would push their thinking around social justice and build on skills that they learned during their school day in a fun and interactive manner.

Because "The Little Mermaid" was being remade with Halle Bailey as Ariel, Joanna and Marika felt it would be great to fold this into the mix by celebrating diversity and the fact that a Black actress was being cast in the lead role. Representation matters, and we wanted the students to feel connected to this initiative. This proved to be a successful strategy. Students from various racial and gender backgrounds created some mermaid-inspired articles of clothing for the American Girl doll baskets using donated sewing kits and templates.

Volunteers Laura Fonte, Pauline MacLellan and Deanna Sklenak shared their sewing expertise with the students, bringing a "home economics" feel to this after-school program.

The vision comes to life!

The big day finally arrived when the American Girl dolls were sold, along with other donated items including antiques, furniture and artwork, at Joanna's house. Marika (right) and Gena Thompson, a parent of one of the Boston-resident students, delivered American Girl doll baskets — given new life through the hard work of the students and volunteers — and also drove students to the house so they could arrange their "products" and sell, sell, sell!

Dr. Sharon Hobbs (center), principal of grades 5–8 in Lincoln, also helped transport and chaperone students. It was a very good day! The students were enthusiastic, learning the art of negotiation and demonstrating excellent customer service — and the MCC raised over $2,500 from the American Girl Doll sales.

Estate sales become a big part of the MCC picture

While suucessfully refurbishing and selling American Girl dolls, we began collecting donations of estate-sale items. These were sold in one of two ways during the project's four years: at three two-day events where we sold smaller items such as china, linens, pottery, art prints, décor and other lower-priced items (netting a total of $7,500), and a continuous estate sale at Joanna's house, where we sold larger, higher-dollar items. We spread the word that we would take almost anything of value — picking it up in Big Bertha, and giving the donor a signed, itemized 501(c)(3) receipt on the spot — and the donations really started rolling in — including 15 dining room sets.

Bob Kupperstein and Spencer Burton of Lincoln after packing up some of the early estate sale donations.

Another successful sale in the rear-view mirror!

A retired gynecologist and his wife purchased a 10,000-square-foot church on the ocean for their forever home, and they furnished it with several pieces from the continuous MCC estate sale, including an antique sideboard. But the doctor also donated an item of his own — his father's antique proctoscope! Every fine home should have at least one, right? Jeff Witt and his wife Carol agreed — they bought the proctoscope and displayed it in their Victorian red-brick mansion as a curiosity of the Victorian era.

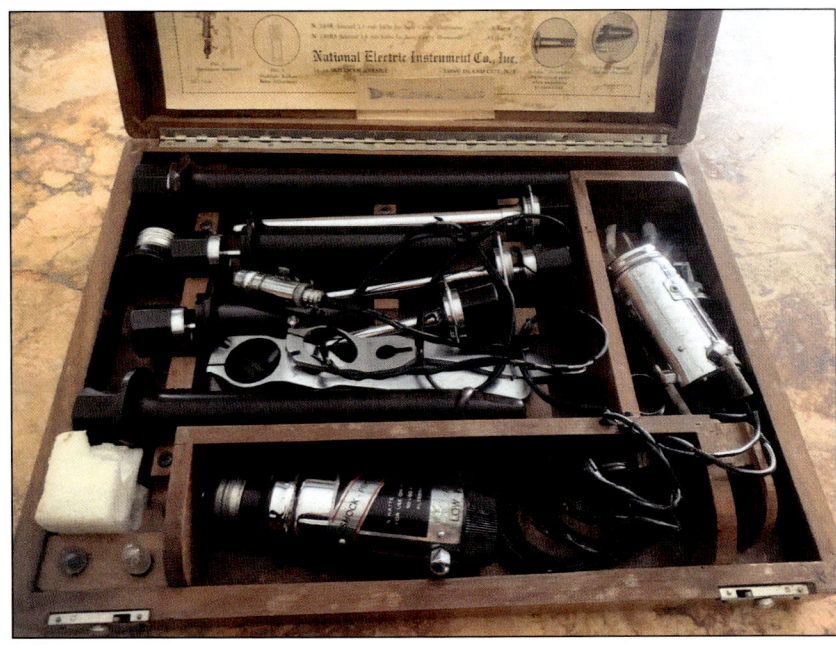

The proctoscope in its wooden box, complete with helpful instructions on the inside lid. Left: its proud new owner, Jeff Witt.

The former and present homes of the antique electrically powered proctoscope (ouch).

You want dolls? We got dolls!

Dozens of Barbie dolls were donated, but how much to charge for them? At a Northeast Doll and Bear Sales show, Joanna met a Barbie consignment expert who coached her on exactly how to price the collection. Then it sold almost right away to a single buyer who drove up from Virginia in his van in winter (Joanna and Erica Gonella had to help shovel him out when he got stuck in the snowy driveway).

SOLD!
300 Barbies for $1,600

The $800 dolls that still give Erica night terrors

Shipping tips

#1: Just don't. Shipping is way too labor-intensive! Only do this for big-dollar purchases, but try to avoid shipping those too!

#2: If you do have to ship something and it's fragile, it's a good idea to communicate with your buyer through-out the process as to how you are packaging and shipping. Use pictures! It builds trust with the buyer and may offer you some legal protection if the product gets broken en route.

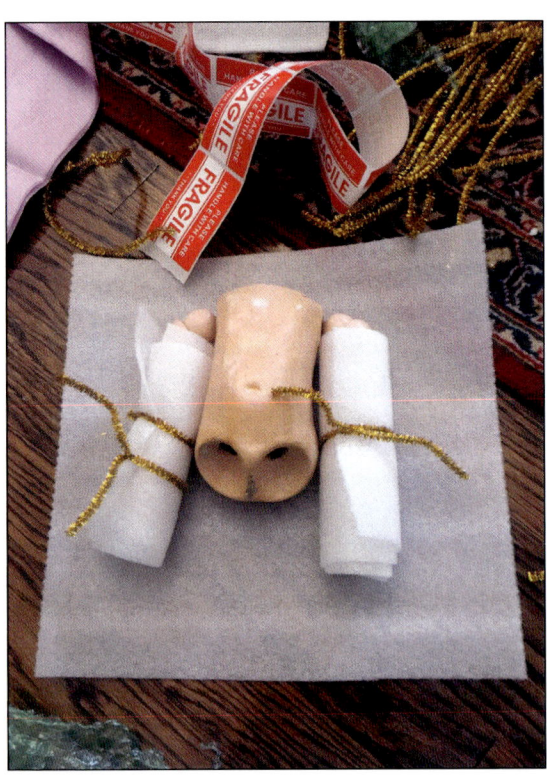

Kimono my house, my house...

Greg Schmergel served as a fashion model for three separate donations of antique Japanese kimonos. "The model stands 6 feet tall and is appropriately proportioned."

The antique Persian rug that came with "tenants"

MCC team member and rug expert Heather Ring discovered some stowaways in this rug: live moth larvae! (not uncommon, just undesirable). Heather learned about rugs in Turkey and from her grandmother, an avid collector. She grew up surrounded by antique Persian rugs passed down through the generations. Her knowledge has been invaluable in terms of pricing, inspecting, and not being taken advantage of by potential rug buyers.

Rug rats: Heather (the "rug whisperer") and Joanna spent 10 straight hours cleaning her antique Persian rug. We do NOT recommend this — lower the price and let the buyer have it cleaned!

Heather's tips for inspecting, valuing and pricing rugs

- Always inspect the rug! Get down on the floor and crawl around on the rug, looking at both sides (the flashlight on a cell phone is great for extra light).

- The back side can tell you many things. Is there a tag with information on it? Is there evidence of moths/larvae? Look for easy-to-see signs of egg casings and cocoons.

- Are there bare/worn spots on the rug? Look at those closely — do they indicate an ongoing problem like moths or are they actual wear spots?

- If the rug is on the floor in a donor's home, where is it? Look closely for damage when the rug is at an outside door or under an eating area.

- Beware of rugs that are already rolled up/or shrink-wrapped — there could be plenty of problems hiding inside!

- Common rug patterns can easily be identified online, and eBay offers good pricing ideas.

- When handling rugs, don't wear your favorite cashmere sweater, just in case the rug has tenants.

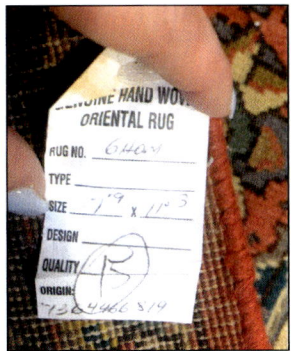

And thank you to Thornton Ring, Heather's husband and Chief Engineer of Getting Singer Sewing Machines Unstuck from their Cabinets!

1950s Herig Persian Rug fetched $600 minus $75 in cleaning supplies for a profit of $525.

A gut feeling was "key" to this sale

SOLD! $3,500

CERTIFICAT DE GARANTIE
CERTIFICATE OF GUARANTEE
AUSSTELLUNG DES GARANTIESCHEINS

PLEYEL

PARIS
depuis 1807

"The generous DiCicco family of Lincoln donated this very special Pleyel piano freighted over from Paris about 20 years ago. I had just a few days to sell it," Joanna says. "I called about 13 potential buyers in Massachusetts on a Sunday. Two called me back that day and it led to a bidding war. I had a bad gut feeling about one of the bidders and I stopped the bidding to sell it to the other buyer.

"So Monday comes and all the other buyers I had left messages with called me back about purchasing the Playel Piano. When they found out it was sold, several of them said, 'Well, as long as you didn't sell it to X!' This was the bidder I had a bad feeling about. Long story short, I made the right call. Go with your gut!"

Piano donor Suzanne DiCicco

Beware of pianos

In 99.9% of cases you will lose a LOT of money if you accept a piano donation. This one was 20 years old, pristine, considered the "Steinway" of Europe, and had been tuned every single year. Unless a buyer is willing to go to the donor's home and move it and pay you on the spot, you should not accept piano donations. Pianos MUST be moved by professional piano movers — always!

! tip

Another sale on the books

Franklin Library "Greatest Books of All Time" collection with leather bindings and with gold leaf (97 of the 100 books)

Collectors are *very* serious about the care, packaging and transport of their collection purchases and the accuracy with which you describe them. These books had never been opened. Notice how we never fully opened them when taking pictures. We didn't want to break, crease or in any way change the condition of the books from "never opened" to "opened." Why? A serious collector will notice!

Bijoy Misra, who purchased the books on behalf of the nonprofit India Discovery Center for $699.

Asking for donations via
e-commerce and online communities
Patch.com

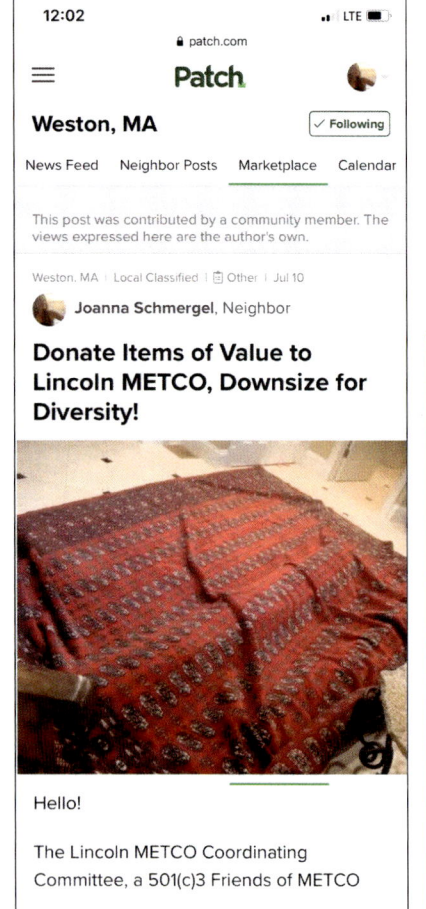

12:02 ··· LTE ▮

🔒 patch.com

Patch.

Weston, MA ✓ Following

News Feed | Neighbor Posts | Marketplace | Calendar

This post was contributed by a community member. The views expressed here are the author's own.

Weston, MA | Local Classified | 🗓 Other | Jul 10

👤 **Joanna Schmergel**, Neighbor

Donate Items of Value to Lincoln METCO, Downsize for Diversity!

Hello!

The Lincoln METCO Coordinating Committee, a 501(c)3 Friends of METCO

Online advertising tip #1

Advertise in 35 nearby towns for two days to get maximum coverage and stay under $100 per item.

---

organization here in Lincoln, MA, is seeking donations of estate items of value.

We will come to your home and pick them up in our truck and give you our signed, itemized 501(c)3 receipt on the spot!

We have taken just about everything of value so it never hurts to ask!

Call Joanna Schmergel at 617-645-9059 to schedule a pick up!

100% of all profits goes towards our goal of reaching $100k in net estate sales by August 2021.

This will allow us to set up a policy-governed investment fund that will start to pay for Lincoln METCO school year programs in perpetuity!

We started this estate sale fundraiser in August of 2017, and even with 9 COVID shutdown months, we are currently at net estate sales of $97,918!!

Our Vision:

The MCC supports building a strong, anti-racist community in which students and families with different life experiences feel a deep sense of inclusion and belonging and recognize, accept, and celebrate each other's differences. We also support the METCO program by activating caregivers to help attain its goals and priorities.

Our Mission:

We will achieve our vision by:

Creating opportunities for Lincoln resident and Boston resident students and caregivers to build authentic and lasting relationships and an equitable exchange of welcoming experiences in both Boston and

---

Lincoln (e.g., opportunities for social connection, after school programming for children, summer camp)

Supporting the school and community in its Anti-racism, Inclusion, Diversity and Equity (AIDE) work (e.g., district NCBI training, caregiver education)
Advocating and supporting the METCO program at both a State and Local level

Organizing resources (funding, volunteers) in support of the METCO team with their work

Advocating for conditions that will promote a truly integrated public school environment (e.g. inclusive curriculum, vision for integration, etc.)

Learn about the Lincoln METCO Coordinating Committee here:

https://lincolnmcc.org/

Please call Joanna Schmergel to schedule a donation pick up today at 617-645-9059!

Downsize for Diversity!!

Warmly,

The Lincoln METCO Coordinating Committee
Joanna Schmergel
Downsize for Diversity!

Lincoln MA Public Schools

owenjoanna@yahoo.com
617-645-9059
Yes We CAN!

See less

〉 **Contact this poster directly**

Freecycle.org

Online advertising tip #2

You can post in up to eight towns (groups) at once, but use slightly different subject lines in each one so the system doesn't ping them as duplicates.

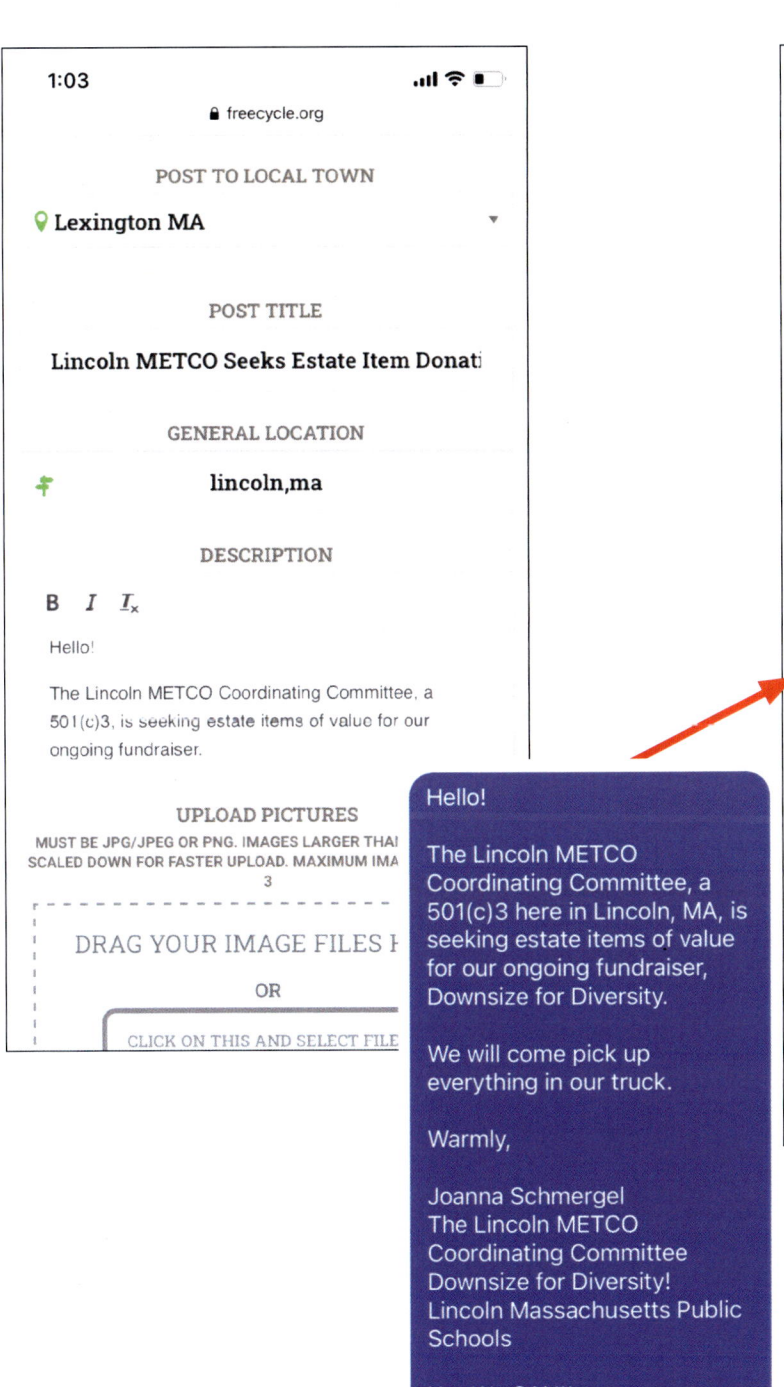

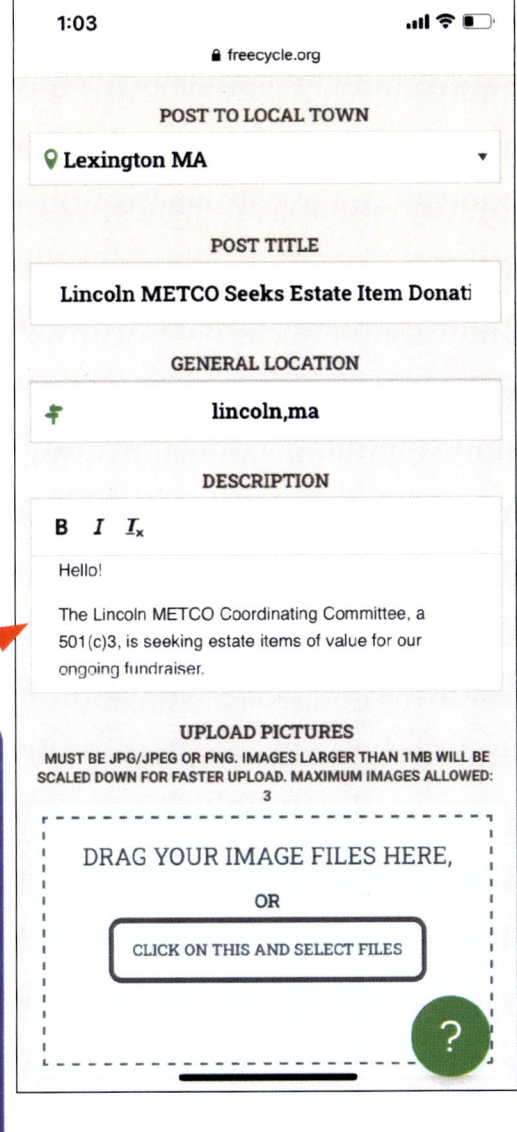

27

Facebook Marketplace

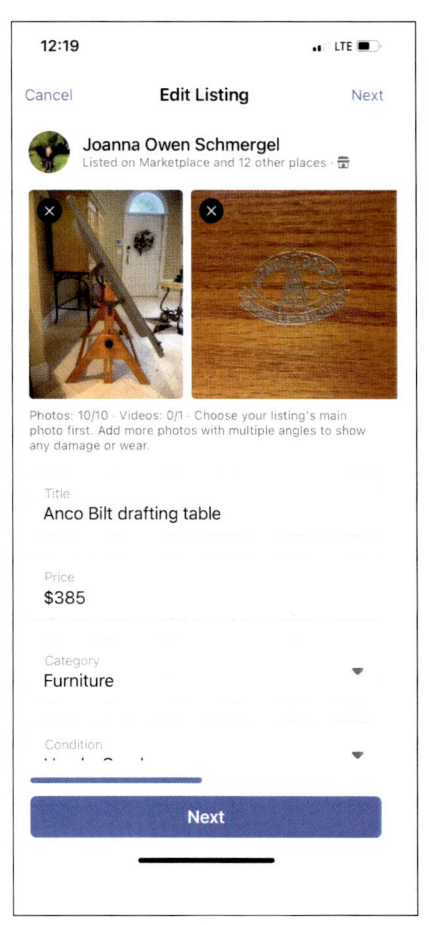

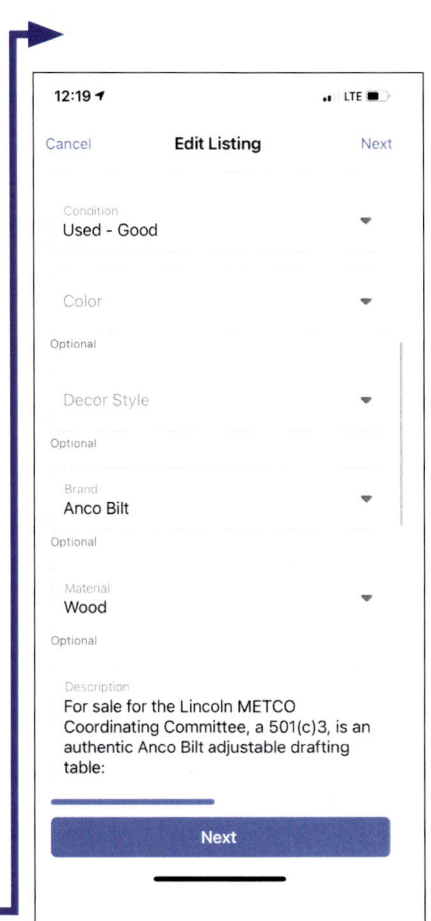

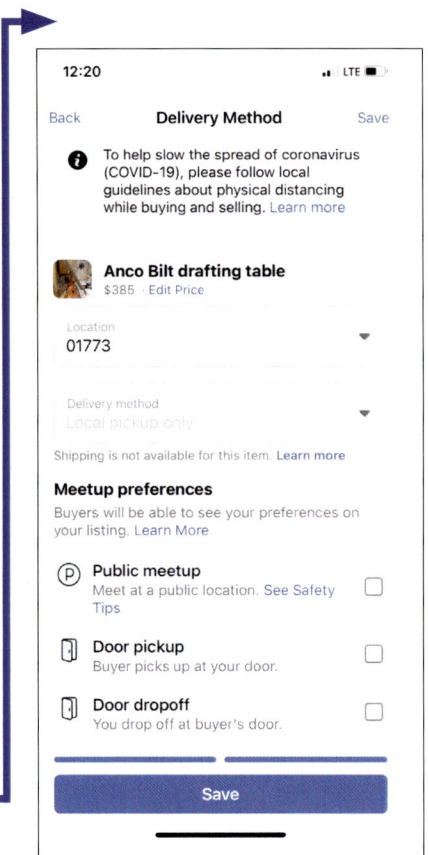

Craigslist.com

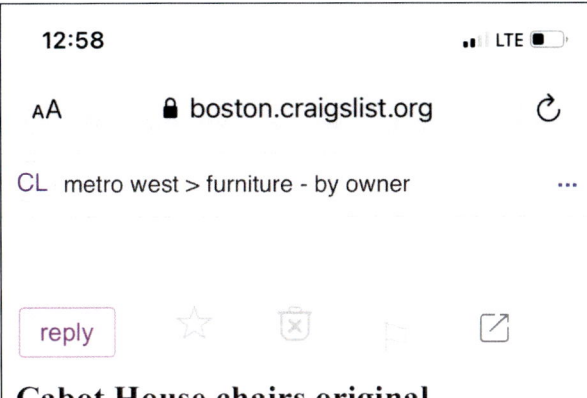

12:58   .ıl LTE

AA   🔒 boston.craigslist.org   ↻

CL metro west > furniture - by owner   ...

reply ☆ 🗑 ⚑ ↗

Cabot House chairs original upholstery - $285 (Lincoln Massachusetts)

For sale for the Lincoln METCO Coordinating Committee, a 501(c)3, is a pair of Baker chairs from Cabot House with original upholstery. They were purchased in 2005 for $3,500 each by the very generous Lincoln donor

We are shutting down next week for flu season so if you want it please purchase and pick up before Tuesday October 6th by close of business!

Measurements:

Width: 35"
Length: 32"
Height: 36"
Floor to Seat Height: 18"

1 chair has a few tiny fabric tears on the arm creases on both arms. These are not noticeable and covered by the

---

12:58   .ıl LTE

🔒 boston.craigslist.org

The other chair has the same on just 1 arm.

1 chair has a rust colored stain very low on the inner side of the arm. This is completely covered by the seat cushion.

100% of all profits goes towards our goal of reaching $100k in net estate sales by May 2021.

This will allow us to set up a policy-governed investment fund that will start to pay for Lincoln METCO school year programs in perpetuity!

We started this estate sale fundraiser in August of 2017 and we are currently at net estate sales of $78,409!!

Social distancing and PPE strictly enforced.

Downsize for Diversity!!

Warmly,

Joanna Schmergel
The Lincoln METCO Coordinating Committee
Fundraising Lead
Lincoln Massachusetts Public Schools

https://www.lpto.org/metco-coordinating-committee

Yes We CAN!!

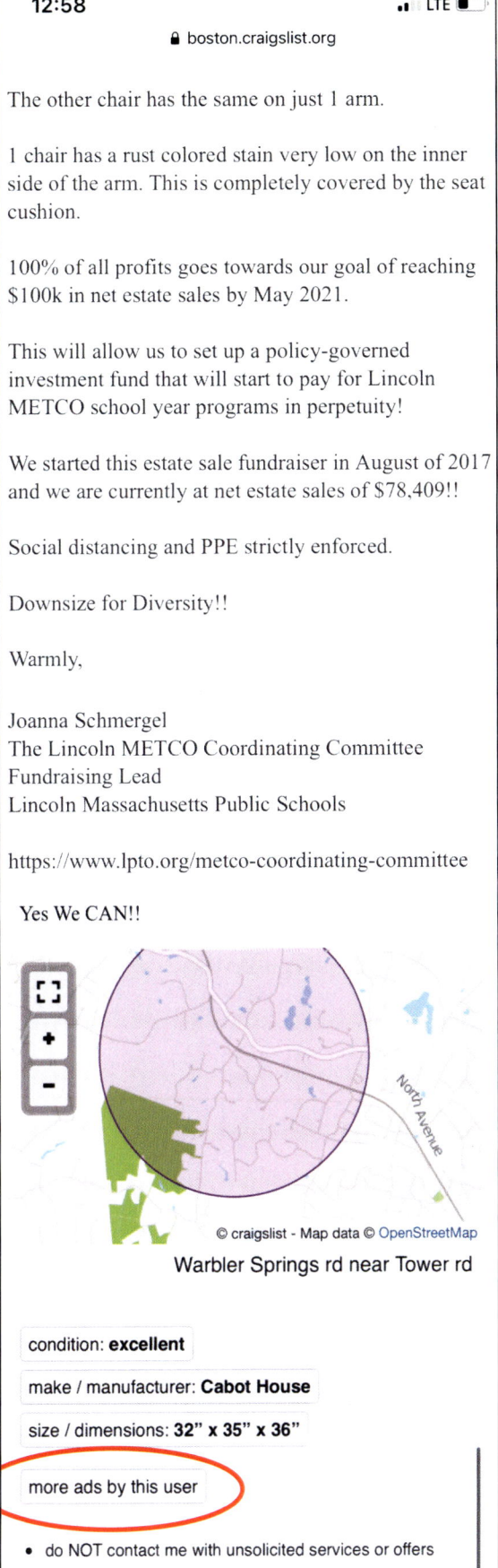

© craigslist - Map data © OpenStreetMap

Warbler Springs rd near Tower rd

condition: **excellent**

make / manufacturer: **Cabot House**

size / dimensions: **32" x 35" x 36"**

more ads by this user

- do NOT contact me with unsolicited services or offers

Online advertising tip #3

Always select "More ads by this user" so people can see everything you have for sale.

LincolnTalk.org

(LincolnTalk is a free subscription email listserv for Lincoln residents.)

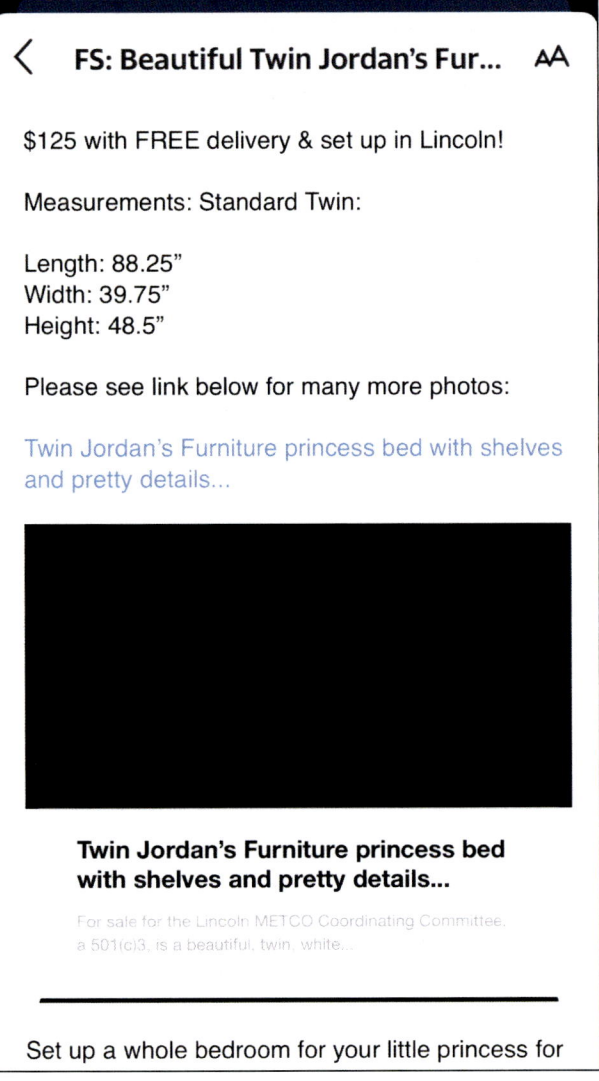

FS: Beautiful Twin Jordan's Fur... AA

Set up a whole bedroom for your little princess for a small fraction of the price with these other items in the photos also for sale:

4 post twin Jordan's Furniture princess bed with all parts: $125

Pair of Cabot Furniture fabric chairs with custom upholstery, originally $3,500 each, just $285 for the pair!

Original acrylic by lauded artist, Francesca Luca, A Morning by the Sea, $165

Original acrylic by lauded artist, Francesca Luca, Full of Life, $155

100% of all profits goes towards our goal of reaching $100k in net estate sales by April 2021.

This will allow us to set up a policy-governed investment fund that will start to pay for Lincoln METCO school year programs in perpetuity!

We started this estate sale fundraiser in August of 2017 and we are currently at net estate sales of $83,572!!

Please call Joanna Schmergel to view or purchase at 617-645-9059.

Social distancing and PPE strictly enforced.

Downsize for Diversity!!

Warmly,

The Lincoln METCO Coordinating Committee

Joanna Schmergel
The Lincoln METCO Coordinating Committee
Fundraising Lead
Lincoln Massachusetts Public Schools
617-645-9059

https://www.lpto.org/metco-coordinating-committee

Yes We CAN!!

| Delete | Archive | Move | Reply | More |

SOLD!

The tale of the runaway pouf

This Restoration Hardware leather ottoman pouf worth $1,000 was one of the project's earlier pickups, but it took two trips to get it home. Joanna loaded it into Big Bertha along with some other stuff but when she got home, it was nowhere to be found. Turns out the pouf was not securely tied down. She retraced her steps and found some of her bungee cords lying on the train tracks at the railroad crossing on Route 117 in Lincoln. She then put out a plea for the missing pouf on the LincolnTalk email listserv and by chance, a fellow Lincolnite had seen it several miles away on the side of Route 27 in Sudbury. A Sudbury police officer helped her carefully retrieve it during rush hour. "It's a really nice one!" he commented.

Joanna's children Gage and Aurora test the pouf's comfort level.

Donor Nick Morgan poses with the recovered pouf.

Packing tip #1

Buy two packs of 24 multi-length carabiner-style bungee cords. These work the best!

A Charlestown pickup during a monsoon

...in which we learn that mahogany bubbles when wet

Packing tip #2

- Always pack tarps and a big roll of furniture shrinkwrap.
- Rub down wet wood with beeswax wood polish and conditioner if it gets wet or scratched.

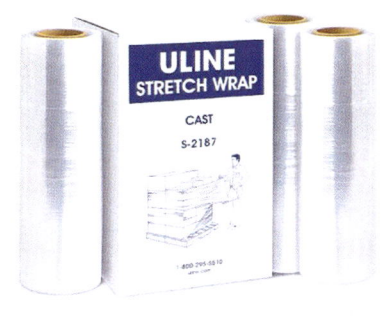

The Lincoln MCC 501(c)(3) form for donors

Leave both dollar-value lines blank for the donor to complete.

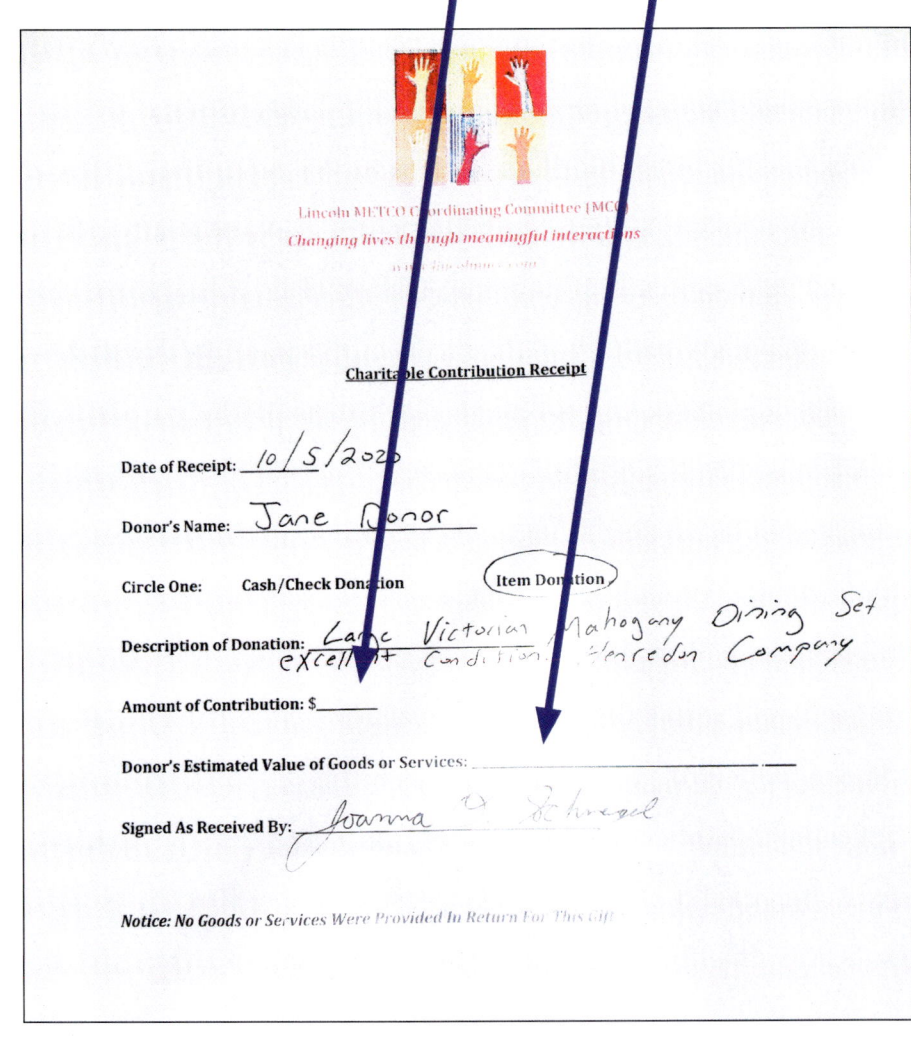

Our first donation pickup that required professional movers

Hector introduced Joanna to one of his clients, Maggie Hunt at Hunt Estate Sales and a very profitable partnership. Maggie runs a company in Chestnut Hill that manages very high-end estate sales for residential clients. She will often call us up to come at the tail end of a sale and allow us to choose from the best of the unsold items. We then give her clients a 501(c)(3) form for their donations.

Above: Hector Mendez and his moving team. He had helped Maggie Hunt for many years and was a huge help to the MCC team in planning and moving large items. Joanna's relationship with Hector came full circle in the end when the MCC received the huge Drew/Berry windfall donation (see page 83). This took us from $98,000, well over our $100,000 goal to $123,000. Without Hector's unique small-move, low-cost business, we probably could not have afforded movers for that job.

Maggie Hunt, Hunt Estate Sales
617-817-1178
huntestatesales.com

Visual aids for spreading the MCC estate sale message

Donate estate items to Lincoln METCO!

- Free pickup for high-value estate items (loadable by one person)
- Signed 501(c)3 receipts on the spot

Goal: a $100,000 fund to pay for Lincoln METCO activities in perpetuity

Call Joanna Schmergel to schedule pickup at 617-645-9059

An ad in the Lincoln Sauirrel, Lincoln's online newspaper.

Schedule a Pickup Today!
617-645-9059

DOWNSIZE for DIVERSITY!

Donate Estate Items of Value

Lincoln METCO Coordinating Committee 501(c)3

Lincoln, MA Public Schools K-8

Joanna Schmergel, Fundraising Lead

18 Cerulean Way, Lincoln, MA 01773

617-645-9059 to donate estate items of value!

owenjoanna@yahoo.com

Business cards with Joanna's contact information for potential donors and buyers

Our new Downsize for Diversity logo designed and created by Lincoln student Anna Lucchese.

A dragon logo created by the daughter of the donor of an elaborate bed solely for use by the MCC.

Planning ahead for three Lincoln pickups in one day

The MCC oftentimes had to move large or heavy items, but they didn't have the budget to hire big-dollar movers. Fortunately, they found Hector Mendez (see page 35) and Charlie Frumkin, an industrious high school student who was running a summer business called Charlie's Garage Cleanouts (781-492-5009) and advertised his services on LincolnTalk. His pickup and trailer as well as his muscles were invaluable when we had to make three pickups in a single day.

Packing tip #3

Take the time to unload and re-load for optimal safety and security of your items, even if it's 100 degrees out in July and you're in masks. We had a sleigh bed that almost slipped off Joanna's truck!

Nick Soukup helped pack one of the three truckloads.

For heavy loads, "weight" and get help

Loading and transporting a very heavy cast iron Ben Franklin stove with decorative screen needed planning and teamwork.

Abigail Adams, Erica Gonella, Nick Soukup and Joanna Schmergel worked together, lifting ergonomically and fashioning a ramp to get the stove onto the truck.

Mysterious cabinet houses servers with a smile

One of our more unusual donations was a big metal cabinet similar to the one at left that was gifted to us by The Food Project, another Lincoln nonprofit. We intially thought it was an ice cream freezer but quickly learned it was actually a Liebert computer server rack.

Hector once again saved the day by advising and helping move this very heavy item. We were able to sell it partly because Joanna was thorough about photographing the maintenance log and various other informational labels.

The server rack sold for $500, resulting in a profit of $290 after subtracting $210 for moving labor.

Do your delivery research

- Always research the job if you are not sure of the weight or complexity of the move. This item required Hector and his team or else we would have gotten hurt.
- Offering free delivery with high-dollar sales can help you sell large items and turn over inventory fast.

Big Bertha's packing list for any pickup

- A double-size camping sleep mat
- Sleeping bags
- Moving blankets
- Old patio cushions
- Two sets of carabiner bungee cords
- Phillips & flathead screwdrivers
- Small and medium-size sturdy boxes
- Packing tape
- Rope
- A socket wrench set
- A first aid kit and water
- Packing paper and cardboard boxes
- A shiv and hammer in case old furniture bolts are embedded in wood
- Measuring tape
- Scissors
- A rubber-headed mallet to gently knock bedrails loose from frames
- Blank 501(c)3 receipts and pens
- Personal protective gear
- Two rolling pallets

A beautiful array of items from Southeast Asia

Concord resident Hester Schnipper grew up all over Southeast Asia and collected many pieces of art and furniture over the years. She donated almost a dozen valuable items, including a dining set that once seated her father (a three-star general in the U.S. Army) and President Dwight D. Eisenhower during a dinner at West Point. There aren't enough pages in this book to showcase all of her amazing donations.

Antique Vietnamese basket used to carry live ducks to market.

Vintage Samoan Siapo barkcloth art.

Hester Schnipper and Mattia Gentile (right), the Schmergels' au pair from southern Italy,

41

An elaborate bed for a second home

Measure twice, load once

If you can, try to polish and take measurements and photos of the items at the donor's location before you load up your vehicle. This way, you can list the item and possibly sell it without ever unloading it from your truck, thus saving yourself an unload and reload.

The buyer, who sent this beautiful bed to his second home in Haiti.

Just a few of our Midcentury Modern donations

The Brookline donor of this piece was one of the original Lincoln METCO host families.

Kathryn Corbin and the "original" oil painting: lessons learned

Joanna posted what she mistakenly described as an original oil painting by J.B.C. Corot for sale on Lincoln-Talk. Kathryn Corbin — who used to be the head of the Paintings Department at Skinner's, the New England auction firm — called her up immediately to say that based on the photo, it was most likely not an oil painting, and if it was by Corot, one of the most important French painters of the nineteenth century, it would be worth $100,000 or more! She came right over, and sure enough, it was a reproduction of a painting by Corot.

Joanna learned how to tell the difference between paintings and prints by their surface, and also that prints can be originals, limited editions or (like this one) a reproduction, all of which can range from rare to merely decorative in value, as was the case here. Thank you, Kathryn!

Kathryn suggests that other Friends of METCO groups would do well to establish relationships with local experts who can help you determine the age, authenticity and value of items that you've been given to sell. They might be a local antiques dealer, collector or auctioneer who would be happy to volunteer their time to help you and other METCO organizations grow this endeavor. No one knows everything, so a go-to roster of experts in different areas will help save you from making costly mistakes or — who knows? — identify a valuable rarity you might have overlooked. What a wonderful surprise that would be!

Kathryn continues to be an important player in the MCC fundraising story, since she recently facilitated a partnership with auction houses Skinners New England & Kaminski's for MCC's pivot to art-only donations.

The J.B.C. Corot picture.

Original art by Francesca Luca

Francesa Luca donated several original paintings to the MCC. "My approach is most concerned with mood, to cultivate an image creating a sense of warmth. With acrylics as my selected medium, I create paintings mostly from my imagination to exude a sense of freedom," she says.

Francesca has had several one-woman shows in the Boston area and her paintings have been exhibited at the Massachusetts General Hospital Cancer Center. Her mail is info@talkwithfrancesca.com.

"Full Bloom"

"Statue of Liberty"

Original art by Elinor White of Lincoln and Sarasota

"Sunrise in Taos" (sold for $135).

"The Memory" (sold for $125).

"Venice View" (sold for $50).

"By the Water" (sold for $150).

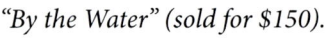

"Peace & Quiet" (sold for $100).

"So Nice to Meet You" (sold for $100).

"The Fence" (sold for $55).

For sale — $65!

More original art donations

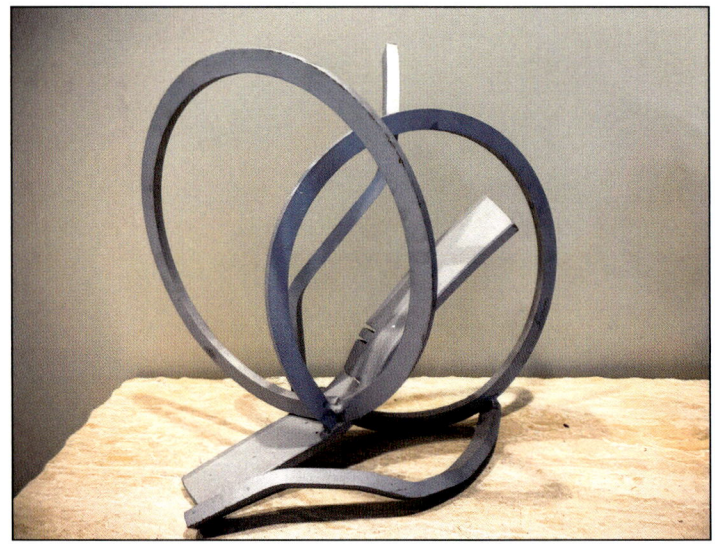

Sculpture by the late David Shapiro of Lincoln (sold for $135).

"Cityscape" a signed original oil painting by Richard Ellis Wagner (sold for $225).

Bowls by Lincoln potter Patty Hilpert (sold for $80 each).

"Newport 1," an original silkscreen by Alejandro Eluchans (sold for $499).

Detail from an Edna Hibel print (sold for $485).

Sculpture by a Pennsylvania farmer who served in the French Foreign Legion (sold for $150).

ZsuZsanna Donnell painting (sold for $375).

"The Black Shed IV" by Alistair Crawford (sold for 699).

Have an eye for detail

Carefully examine the front and back of the picture and its frame for information on the artist, title, when it was created, etc.

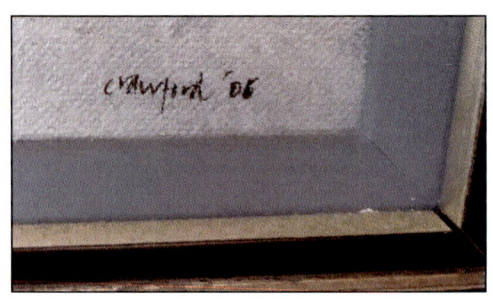

Painting from occupied Japan donated by Hester Schnipper.

"Western Landscape" (sold for $155).

Let's talk about it

Take the time to talk to the donor about their donation, where and when they got it, etc.. This saves a lot of researching time.

This painting was purchased for $75 by a buyer who was smitten with one of Joanna's au pairs when he came to the house to pick it up. Unfortunately she did not return his affection.

Mark is in 3rd Grade in Lincoln Schools. He was born in The Netherlands and moved to Lincoln when he was in kindergarten. He always had a fascination with paints and drawing, spending hours in front of a table full with crayons. He is very proud to invite you to his very first exhibition.
Contact: ruxandra_darie@yahoo.com

EXPO: **April 26th - May 26th**

Dear Friend,

I have the pleasure of inviting you to see my first painting exhibition. I worked and painted for about half a year. I started painting when I was seven with mommy. Lets say I have a bit of experience ☺! I wonder if people are liking my paintings when they do see them. I am a bit nervous but also excited too, for what's to come. I feel pretty lucky for a 9 year old to have an exhibition and when I see my friends coming to look at my paintings
It's like a miracle.

Mark Darie

These beautiful painings were done by Mark Durie, a very talented boy here in Lincoln, when he was just 8 and 9 years old. They're priced at $200 but haven't been posted for sale as of late fall 2021, as we shut down for "COVID Meets Flu Season."

A very generous and interesting woman came over to see this beautiful antique mahogany table with exquisite herringbone inlay from Rothchild's in New Orleans. We were asking $1,500. After asking us many questions about Downsize for Diversity, she tapped her executive employee Fidelity charity account and made a $4,000 donation for the table!

The donated table in Joanna's house (above), and after delivery and setup in the buyer's house (below).

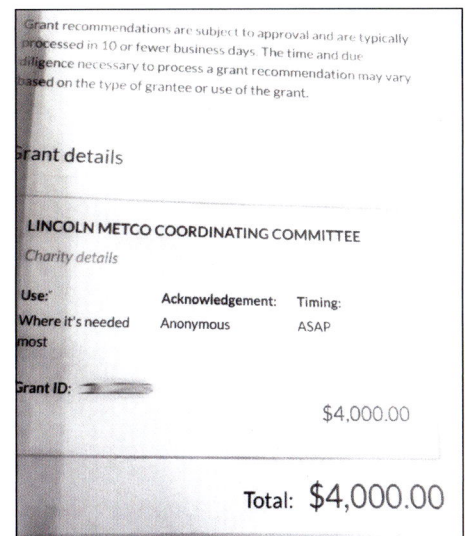

Grant recommendations are subject to approval and are typically processed in 10 or fewer business days. The time and due diligence necessary to process a grant recommendation may vary based on the type of grantee or use of the grant.

Grant details

LINCOLN METCO COORDINATING COMMITTEE
Charity details

Use:*	Acknowledgement:	Timing:
Where it's needed most	Anonymous	ASAP

Grant ID:

$4,000.00

Total: $4,000.00

The diversity of donations

At an event hosted by the First Parish of Lincoln and the MCC, Joanna told Milly Arbaje-Thomas, President and CEO of Boston METCO, that we would sell anything people were willing to donate — even a boat. By an amazing coincidence, the very next week a Lincoln resident donated this 17-foot Penobscot Bay canoe and accessories that we sold for $450!

Packing up a pair of four-posters

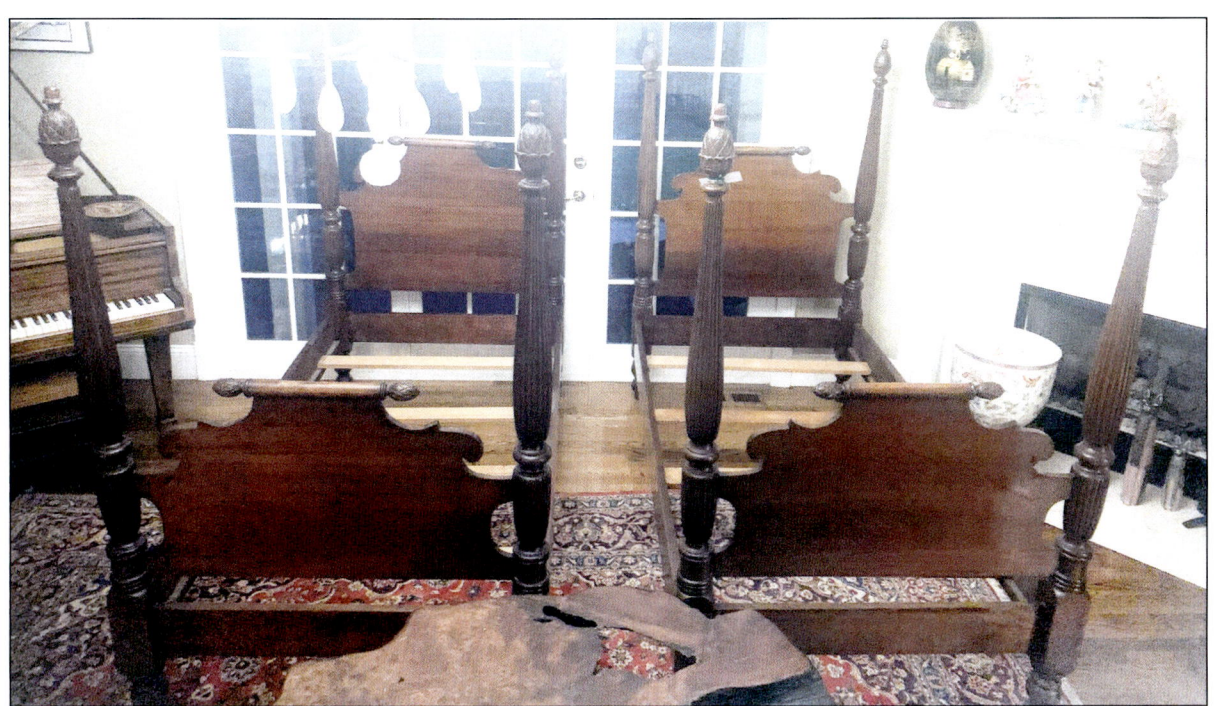

A happy customer buys twin antique four-poster mahogany beds for his daughters.

Laszlo teaches Joanna how to sand and stain

Sanding and staining

- Use a 100% cotton cloth to stain, not a brush.

- Remove drawers first.

- Do not use an electric sander on delicate parts — use a handheld manual sanding block.

- Don't want to sand and stain? No problem! Sell "as is" and just lower the price!

A refinished Pottery Barn dining set (sold for $700).

A win for a gecko as well as the MCC

A kindergarten teacher who needed to rehome her leopard gecko named Kitty gave it to a fellow teacher in special education in the Sharon Public Schools. But the new owner didn't have the supplies she needed to keep him alive in her clasroom, so she had to remove him from the school and take him to her house.

MCC to the rescue! The teachers all chipped in to buy $500 worth of donated gecko supplies for only $80 for the teacher, saving the animal's life. "All of our students are super excited and they're really looking forward to having their gecko back," she said.

Communicating with donors and buyers

There are many reasons donors may be moving and/or downsizing. Several of these reasons are not always happy. Always be kind. Here are some "sensitive communication" tips from Joanna and Desmond Crowley.

A downsizing donor from Essex, Mass.

Bungee master Desmond Crowley

Sensitivity training

- Clarify with the donor that you are going to pick and choose what you take. Otherwise you'll have a storage problem!

- If listing an imperfect item, take closeup photos of all flaws and mention them in the listing

- Don't check out other items in the donor's home and ask if they would donate them as well.

- If you can't take a certain donation due to size and/or sellability, be very tactful.

- Be very respectful of donors' and buyers' homes.

- Have some understanding of what you can and cannot take before you show up.

- Sometimes donors and buyers can't help you load or unload. Discuss this first and plan ahead for the necessary labor.

- Always specify in writing that all sales are final and all items are sold in "as is" condition.

When buyers are also donors

A wonderful, worldly rabbi from Roslindale bought this beautiful antique Victorian bed along with new bed slats custom-made by handyman Laszlo Hegedus. Then she donated a valuable print from her own collection. This ending up happening a lot — more than a few buyers became donors at delivery.

This bed sold for $600; after subtracting $180 for making the custom slats, MCC'S net profit was $420.

Have the right tools

A good socket wrench set like this one is very necessary for unscrewing bolts in antique beds and other furniture. It's wise to keep one set in your home and one in your vehicle. (See also page 40.)

Sometimes commitment isn't glamorous...

…It's hefting a several hundred pound Edwardian buffet up a 3-floor walk-up in Melrose, with low ceilings, covered in perimenopausal sweat in August….

Loading tips

- When preparing to load anything with drawers, either remove all the drawers and pack and load separately, or wrap the drawers tightly all the way around with shrink-wrap and load the piece with the drawers facing inward on your vehicle.

- A double camping mat is perfect for sliding furniture in and out of your truck. It protects the furniture and your back. It's a good idea to put a hole in the end and secure it to your truck as Joanna's was stolen three times!

The value of intact upholstered furniture

Cabot House Hancock & Moore leather sofa and leather reclining chair (sold for $900).

Two custom Cabot House chairs (sold along with an old Paine's Furniture custom chair for $440).

A Roche Bobois living room set.

The importance of staging

Make the item look attractive and enticing to the buyer by arranging it in such a way that they can imagine it in their own home or in a way that gets their creative juices flowing. Place it next to other beautiful items… use stylish angles… add some pretty fresh flowers in the background.

Safety first!

When our generous Watertown donor warned us that there were a lot of steps, we had no idea — wow! When delivering items to buyers, always specify first-floor delivery only.

The proprietor of Siesta Key Outfitters in Florida, which made the volunteer Downsize for Diversity shirts with the neon glow-in-the-dark arm bands at no extra charge. This woman (originally from Russia) loves hearing about Friends of Lincoln METCO. She's also a tough cookie — she sells toilet paper with Donald Trump's image in Florida!

Have a safe move

- Drink plenty of water.
- Wear good shoes.
- Moving furniture is NOT the time to try to squeeze yourself in "those" jeans.
- Have Motrin and a first aid kit in the car.
- Charge your phone.
- Plan appropriate labor for very heavy loads.
- Wear glow-in-the-dark items when loading at night (see above).
- Rest in between jobs.
- It doesn't hurt to stretch and warm up before lifting and moving furniture.

Two-day estate sale events

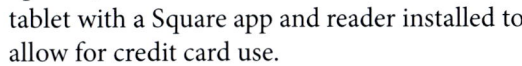

The tiered table for the estate sales event created by Gina.

Tips from Gina Halsted for estate sale events

- Create an ad on Craiglist.com (free) and EstateSales.net ($70).
- Include lots of pictures, descriptions and prices in your ad, particularly of larger, valuable or collectible items.
- Put out lots of signs. Begin at heavily trafficked roads and mark every turn to your sale location. Signs don't have to be fancy — but make sure the print is very large.
- Have numbers available for early birds.
- Consider a two-day event on a Friday and Saturday. We found that 9 a.m. to 3 p.m. works well.
- Designate a "money person" — someone who periodically collects the cash and checks and begins counting/registering them for deposit. Have a safe place to store cash and checks.
- Have one checkout location with at least two checkout volunteers. Each volunteer should have a cash box (with some start-up cash) and an iPhone/ tablet with a Square app and reader installed to allow for credit card use.
- Have lots of bags and boxes available for customers to pack their items.
- Make sure you have a rainy-day backup plan if your sale is outside!
- Try to arrange for a charitable organization to pick up any items that don't sell so you're not trying to find a home for it all.

Donations that run the gamut

We get everything! Some things old and some things new... some that are practical and some just for fun... some for kids and others definitely for the grownups.

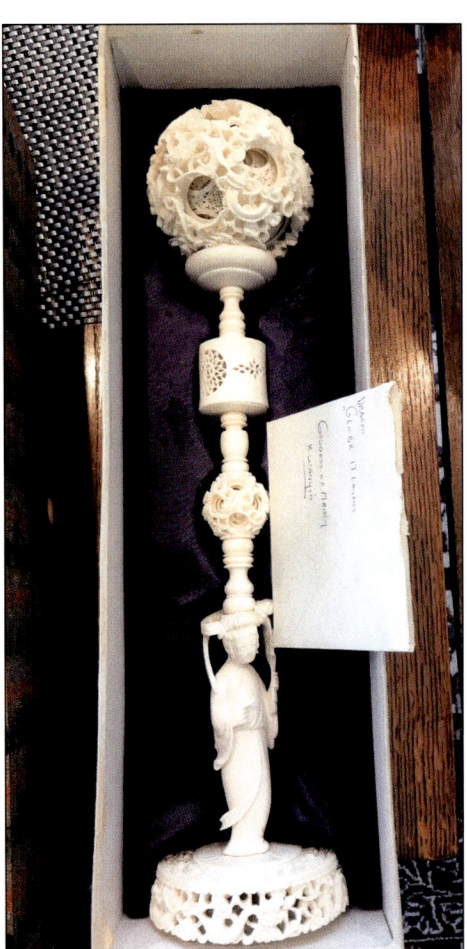

Southeast Asian easel (sold for $145) and an antique carriage horn (sold for $200).

Carved ivory from the 1800s (thus grandfathered and legal), donated by an artist in Lincoln who made sure we knew that we could not sell it outside state lines. The buyer — a Chinese national who purchased the piece for personal reasons, not for resale at a profit — inserted a needle dipped in boiling water into the bottom to verify its authenticity.

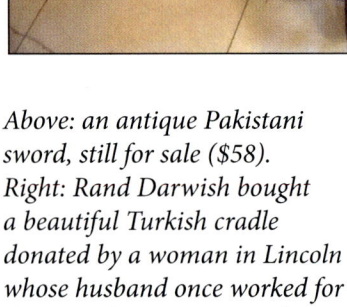

Above: an antique Pakistani sword, still for sale ($58). Right: Rand Darwish bought a beautiful Turkish cradle donated by a woman in Lincoln whose husband once worked for the United Nations in Turkey.

SOLD!
$160

Chinese bronze ritual vessel (sold for $600).

Gage and Aurora Schmergel help stage two train table sets for sales photos.

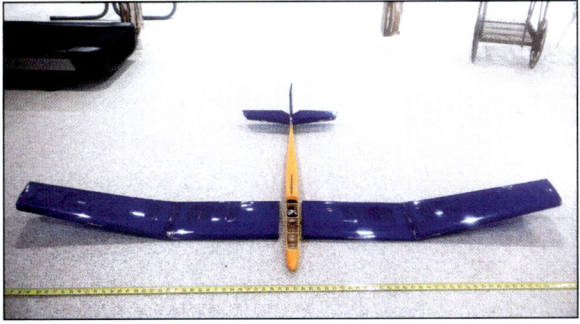

Two radio glider airplanes (sold for $65).

Mahjongg tile game (sold for $99).

A Newton woman donated an Amazonian riverboat totem meant to ward off evil spirits. Her late husband got it as a gift from one of his patients (sold for $265).

A U.S. national soccer team signed jersey (sold for $163).

Our most recent two-day estate sale event brought in $4,000 in net sales... but the best part is that we put a call out for volunteers on LincolnTalk, and Friends of Lincoln METCO members from generations past came forward and stepped up to help!

Peter Pease of Lincoln donates an amazing full drum set (sold for $185).

This Wellesley couple donated two beautiful antique mantle clocks that were eventually purchased by Davida Lowenstein. Turns out she was the MCC treasurer 40 years ago!

It's the Belmont hillbillies!

...Massachusetts, that is!

The Belmont man who donated two beautiful twin antique mahogany four-poster beds (see page 55), a luxury Henredon mahogany sideboard, and at least two high-end rugs, perhaps more…

The last $15K: March–August 2021

...as Downsize for Diversity emerges from the second Covid shutdown

The 18th-century armoire and the Hungarian connection: Laszlo (center) and his fellow handyman Jsort (right) helped us disassemble an 18th-century carved walnut Austrian armoire given by repeat donor Carolyn Gombosi (left) of Newton. Her late Hungarian husband brought it back from Europe. Our anonymous pro bono carpenter recreates the broken foot from scratch. (Incidentally, we know Laszlo though Joanna's Hungarian father-in-law.)

Gretchen Covino volunteers as our model to give the armoire scale and context.

This rug was purchased in China by the father of our generous donor at the end of World War II. He was an Army surgeon who served in China, Burma (Myanmar) and India. He survived the escape from Burma into India, which was similar in both brutality and attrition to the Bataan Death March. You can read about this courageous man in A Surgeon with Stilwell: Dr. John H. Grindlay and Combat Medicine in the China-Burma-India Theater of World War II *by Alan K. Lathrop.*

Pompanoosuc Mills distressed leather sofa (sold for $650).

A custom-carved marble table top purchased in-country by Lincolnite serving as a U.S. Army officer in Turkey (sold for $600).

Original signed pastel portrait from the 1800s of a Lincolnite ancestor (still for sale for $50).

Swan-leg secretary (sold for $225).

She'll take Cara your downsizing

Cara Weir (above left and photo at right) is a professional downsizer with C.E.W. Inc. (617-893-3567) who contacted us because her Lincoln client wanted to donate several pieces of furniture to Lincoln METCO. With her is paid helper Nick Soukup. Below: one of the dining sets she helped move.

Antique Italian inlay table (sold for $250).

Bukhara rug (sold for $749).

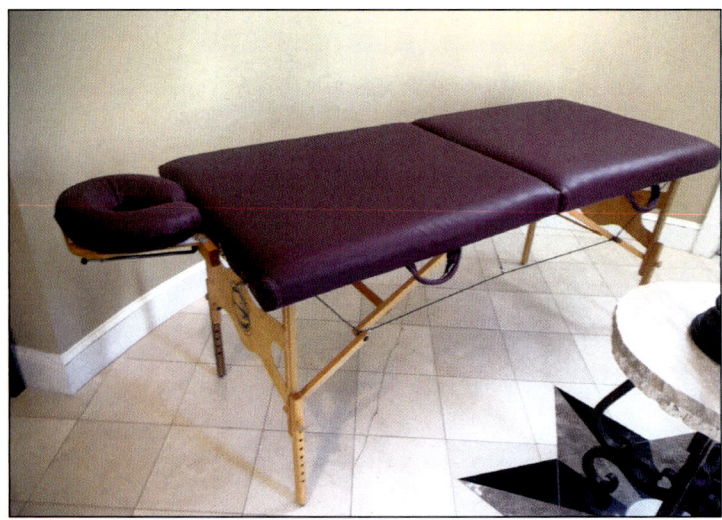

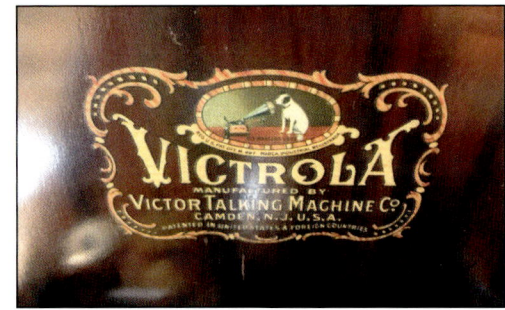

Victrola donated by Catherine Coleman of the Lincoln Cultural Council (sold for $225).

Living Earth massage table (sold for $70).

A former Bedford elementary school principal and his wife (above) donated this oak dropleaf table (sold for $225 after our pro bono carpenter repaired one of the leaves).

A mid-century chinoiserie from a Belmont donor appraised at $7,500 and sold for $625. Many expensive items that were appraised accurately sell for very low prices because demand for them is low, and as a small volunteer-run organization, the MCC only sells locally because of the labor involved in shipping. Right: Desmond Crowley and the Belmont donors.

Artwork by M. Shore (sold for $249).

Liz Suneby of Wellesley, author of "Razia's Ray of Hope" and "Iqbal and His Ingenious Idea," donated a slew of original art. She offered to come to the Lincoln School for free to read her books to the students and talk about them.

Print by V. N. Tonsukh (sold for $50).

"Waiting Women," a lithograph by Federico Sateloon, waiting to sell for $50.

New flower girl dresses donated by Edwina's Bridal, which we donated in turn to South Sudanese Enrichment for Families (another Lincoln nonprofit).

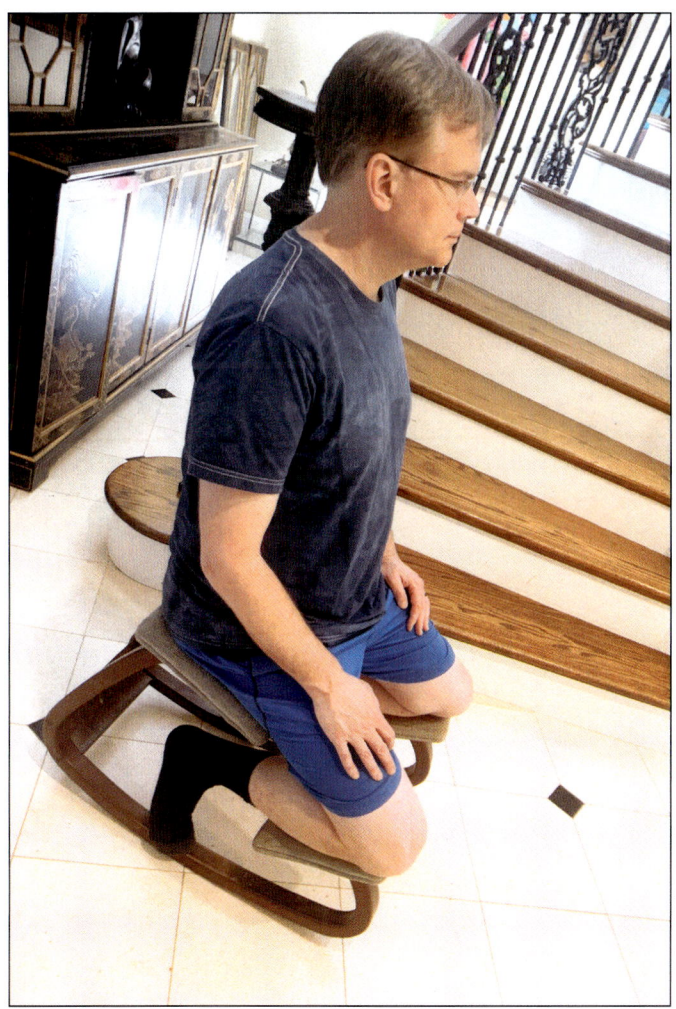

A Lincoln couple donated four "Miss Saigon" theater tickets for which they paid $420. We sold them for $200.

Danish kneeling stool (sold for $25).

Antique French country two-piece secretary (sold for $265).

Black Forest German cuckoo clock (sold for $125).

Dark ivory lace early 1930s christening gown set handmade in Florence, Italy (still for sale at $145).

This Form in Teak dining and console set made in Denmark was sold to this lovely woman for her very swanky Somerville townhouse. While delivering it during a late June heat wave, Joanna remarked, "Wow! I haven't seen Somerville since season 2 of The Handmaid's Tale!" They had a good laugh in the miserable heat. The table, console and eight chairs sold for $975.

This Maggiolini collection armoire and coffee table with marquetry inlay, custom-made in Italy, sold for $235 and $250 respectively.

Detail of armoire door.

Crate & Barrel dining table and bench (sold for $385).

Crate & Barrel dresser (sold for $385).

Jordan's Furniture dresser (sold for $150).

CB2 five-piece patio set sold to Dennis and Jamie Liu for $499.

John Stuart Mid-century Modern chair (sold for $700).

CB2 bed, nightstands and bench (sold for $325).

Marketing on two feet and two wheels

During the summer of 2021, Joanna incorporated walking and biking — while also distributing flyers — into her fitness routine. She hit almost every street in Lincoln! This yielded more donations than any paid advertising could have.

As a bonus, the clown-car horn on her Huffy one-speed beach cruiser bike scared the wild turkeys away.

This mailbox-stuffing marketing strategy led us to the Great Windfall…

Schedule a FREE Pickup Today!
617-645-9059

DOWNSIZE for DIVERSITY!

Donate Estate Items of Value

www.lincolnmcc.org

Lincoln METCO **Coordinating Committee 501(c)3**

Lincoln, MA Public Schools K-8

Joanna Schmergel, Fundraising Lead

18 Cerulean Way, Lincoln, MA 01773

617-645-9059 to donate estate items of value!

owenjoanna@yahoo.com

The Downsize for Diversity business cards and flyer (below) that the MCC papers all over Lincoln and beyond.

Downsize for Diversity!

Donate items of value to Lincoln METCO! Free pick-up in our truck & signed, itemized 501©3 receipts on the spot! $85k raised towards our goal of $100k investment fund to pay for METCO activities in perpetuity. Call Joanna Schmergel to schedule a pick-up at 617-645-9059!

A $25,282 windfall from the Drew/Berry estate

In July 2021, Joanna got a call from one of the homes where she'd left a flyer (see previous page). The call was from Rachel Drew, a Lincoln resident who was helping her husband dispose of the furniture, art and antiques collcted over many years by his mother and stepfather, George and Roberta Berry.

"My in-laws loved to entertain, so their house was well suited to that, with higher-end furnishings and lots of decorative touches that reflected their love of travel, animals, and enjoying time with friends and family," Rachel says.

The family invited some estate auction companies to identify some of the items with higher resale values. "After that, we had quite a few larger furnishings that neither we nor the auction houses had space for, as well as many smaller decorative items that we weren't sure what to do with," Rachel says. "George and Roberta had always been philanthropists and supported many causes, so charitable donations seemed like the natural next step for these items. My husband and I are also big supporters of the METCO program — we both grew up in the Boston suburbs and attended public schools that participated in METCO and knew how valuable the program is, and we greatly appreciate that Lincoln participates so our kids (currently in seventh and tenth grades) can get that same perspective."

Having heard about the Downsize for Diversity program through LincolnTalk, the Lincoln for Families Facebook page, and the mailbox flyer, Rachel invited Joanna over to take a look. After recovering from her astonishment at the numerous valuable and beautiful pieces, Joanna and Gina took photos and measurements and lined up Hector, since this job was far too large and important for Big Bertha.

"Honestly, I was (pleasantly!) surprised at what she

A vintage Japanese carved samurai armoire (sold for $250).

wanted — we had been told some of the larger items would not be of interest to charities because of the cost/hassle to move them, but Joanna said she had movers who could do that (with that cost deducted from the proceeds of the sales), so that was a huge bonus to us. I think a combination of the quantity and quality of items available made it

A pair of Chinese guardian Foo lions. Joanna's husband liked them so much that when they were still for sale on the third day of the event, he bought them for $1,050.

Bird's-eye maple secretary (sold for $885)

worth that expense too," Rachel says.

"After that initial round, I invited Joanna back a second time when we were down to more decorative items, and again she surprised me with the amount she wanted to take — our alternatives at that point were few, so I was just glad that she wanted them and they would not end up in a dumpster (our last resort). So the Downsize for Diversity program actually ended up being a huge help to us as well!"

The sale had to happen fairly quickly, so Joanna mobilized the troops and had Hector pack and move everything in preparation for a special three-day estate sale event at her house about three weeks later. All three of her garage bays had to be cleared out, and the overflow went into her living room, dining room, foyer and front yard. The successful event brought in $25,282, putting Downsize for Diversity over the $100,000 fund-raising goal line.

Hector and his team moved and unloaded the items for temporary storage in our garage and later arranged everything for the sale.

Joanna made notices with rules for the sale and Desmond mounted them on a big board for buyers to see as they came in.

MCC put special flyers up all over Joanna's property with contact information for Hector & the Handy Hands Moving Co. so buyers would have a "go-to" resource to get their items home.

We sold some small-dollar pieces like these ("70 bucks for a pack of seven ducks!") but the vast majority of items at this special luxury sale were priced at more than $150 apiece.

A large red and gold hand-painted hall mirror (sold for $425).

Two Baker Furniture breakfronts (sold for $1,950).

At the suggestion of Maggie Hunt from Hunt Estate Sales, we contacted Lark Mason from Antiques Roadshow. He wrote back within the hour and helped us accurately price all our pieces from Asia for free. Jessica Hull from Exceptional Estate Sales also went through every single item and checked and adjusted our prices (also pro bono). You only get one chance to price items correctly out of the gate at a high-end sales event like this.

A pair of Chinese side tables (sold for $370).

A whimsical glass and iron table with a cast-iron cat and mouse sculpture forming part of the base. Balls of cast-iron "yarn" served as the armrests on the six matching chairs (all sold for $925).

We sold this ultra-heavy monkey bowl for $80. As we were packing it up for the customer, we saw the original price tag for $580 still on the bottom — oops!

Chinese post-World War II long coffee table (sold for $425).

"Henry in Love" (print sold for $110).

Antique reproduction glass-front bookcase (sold for $425).

Set of five chairs with hand-painted silk seats (sold for $1,665).

Sofa table (sold for $785).

Four inlaid coffee tables (sold for $1,165).

Part of a five-piece carved walnut bedroom set that sold for a total of $950.

Heirloom hand-woven Persian rug donated on the day of the sale (sold for $585).

Custom Italian eight-foot sideboard (sold for $589)

Three-piece silk sofa set (sold for $795).

Prince Monyo original sculpture (sold for $2,400).

"Berkshire Winter" original oil on canvas signed by artist B.J. Faulkner (unsold, priced at $725).

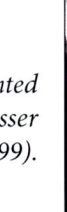

Hand-painted dresser (sold for $299).

Baker dining table (sold for $1,250).

Antique pigeon loft for homing, racing, or acrobatic pigeons (sold for $525).

The MCC's Heather Ring shakes hands with Wayne Ogden, member of the board of directors of METCO, Inc., who volunteered to work on day one of the luxury three-day Drew/Berry sale with his wife Betsy.

Yes we did!

- From August 2017 to August 2021, we raised $122,694 in net estate sales.
- We had another $7,000 in earnings from the investment fund we started about three years into the project. Great work, Rebecca!
- We collected donations from 33 different towns in Massachusetts and 252 different donors.
- We made 655 individual and bulk sales (not including sales during the two-day estate sale events).
- During this four-year period, the effort was shut down for nine months due to the COVID-19 pandemic.

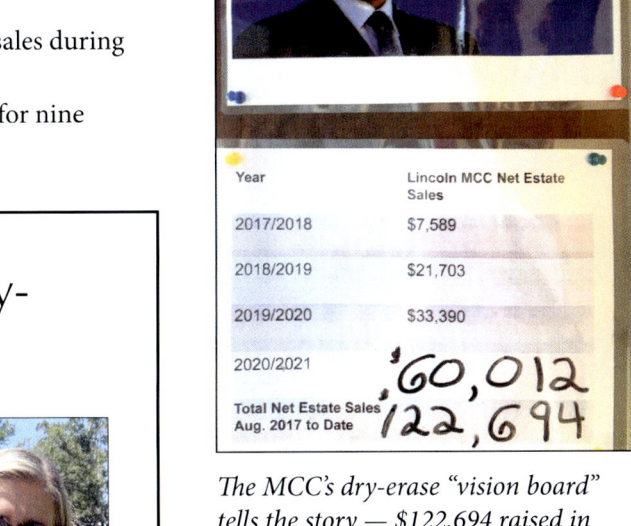

Year	Lincoln MCC Net Estate Sales
2017/2018	$7,589
2018/2019	$21,703
2019/2020	$33,390
2020/2021	$60,012
Total Net Estate Sales Aug. 2017 to Date	$122,694

The MCC's dry-erase "vision board" tells the story — $122,694 raised in just under four years, well above the original $100,000 goal.

The basic rules for our policy-governed investment fund

Compiled by MCC treasurer and chief investment officer Rebecca Blanchfield.

- All transactions are for the sole benefit of Lincoln MCC.
- Passive investing with auto-rebalancing is best.
- Diversify, diversify, diversify!
- No speculative investments or stock pickers — it never ends well!
- Have a long-term investment horizon.
- No more than 4% of the fund can be withdrawn each year.
- The MCC board reviews all fund withdrawals and develops a plan for paying it back within an academic year.

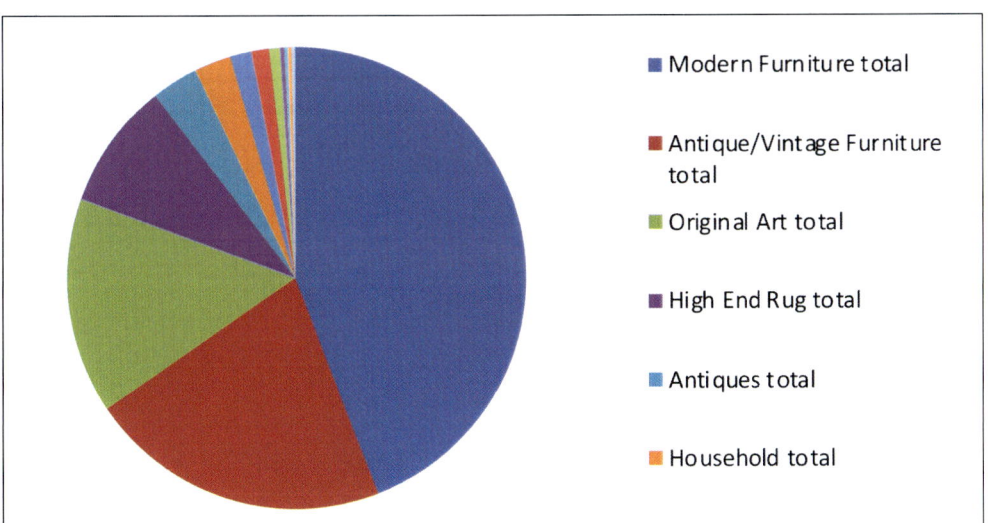

- Modern Furniture total
- Antique/Vintage Furniture total
- Original Art total
- High End Rug total
- Antiques total
- Household total

A breakdown of sales by type of item for the year ending June 30, 2021. The MCC netted $60,000 in sales that year — its most successful year of the four by far, because by then the group had honed their skills and had a good sense of what donations to accept and how to price them for sale.

Record-keeping tips
from treasurer Erica Gonella

- Keep records of which individuals donated in-kind (i.e., non-cash) items and were given a tax receipt.

- Link payment apps like Square or Venmo to your 501(c)3 tax identification number (TIN), not your personal Square or Venmo account, or you will owe taxes personally.

- Favor cash or electronic transactions but if you choose to accept personal checks, deposit them ASAP.

- Each donation should be recorded at the fair market value upon receipt.

- Every non-cash gift should be evaluated to determine its usefulness to the organization. Otherwise, the organization could end up with something that requires a lot of work for little value.

- If you can't research the price, you can rely on a good-faith estimate by the donor if you lack a ready means of independent valuation for things like art work. An independent appraisal is required if the value exceeds $5,000.

- Do not provide anything that documents a value to the donor unless there is a formal appraisal. A thank-you letter can state a description of what was given, but unless there's an appraisal, it's up to the donor to document the value, and the organization should not provide anything that appears to give validity to the value the donor has provided.

Form **1023**	**Application for Recognition of Exemption**	OMB No. 1545-0056
(Rev. December 2017) Department of the Treasury Internal Revenue Service	**Under Section 501(c)(3) of the Internal Revenue Code** ▶ Do not enter social security numbers on this form as it may be made public. ▶ Go to *www.irs.gov/Form1023* for instructions and the latest information.	Note: If exempt status is approved, this application will be open for public inspection.

Tips for achieving 501(c)(3) status with the IRS from Michelle Barnes

- Seek your own tax and legal advice as needed.
- IRS Instructions are clear, follow them to a T – they also have an online minicourse and FAQ for Form 1023.
- You'll first need to apply for an EIN – IRS Form 1023 Instructions show you how.
- You must know the form of your org – likely an "unincorporated association" like us.
- Do you meet the test for using Form 1023EZ? The online instructions for that form include a link to the checklist to find out.
- Remember to file taxes for your nonprofit each year (Form 990 or 990EZ). Failure to file can cause the IRS to revoke your status and then you will need to reinstate it.
- You'll need an organizing document and a narrative description of your activities. Be sure

to include the specific language that is asked for in the Form 1023 instructions — otherwise the process gets prolonged when the IRS asks for corrections (we found out the hard way!).

- Form 1023 requires up to four tax years worth of data on revenues and expenses, as well as the most recent year's balance sheet information.

- Have up to four years of supporting documentation such as bank account statements, brochures, newsletters, fundraising letters and the like.

- You'll learn to love the IRS — really!

Downsize for Diversity in the news

Auction attracts dolls and dollars for Lincoln METCO group

September 12, 2017 by Alice Waugh (Edit)

An unusual but generous donation of vintage dolls will benefit enrichment and recreational programs for the Lincoln School's Boston-based students via the Lincoln's METCO Coordinating Committee (MCC).

The MCC organizes and funds academic and social activities outside of school for Boston and Lincoln students in grades K-8. Lincoln is one of 35 suburban school districts that participates in METCO, the voluntary Boston school desegregation program begun in 1966.

The windfall came about when Lincoln resident Seth Rosen was looking to donate his late mother's large doll collection. His friend Joanna Schmergel—who volunteers in the MCC's after-school kindergarten reading program that connects adult

A Marilyn Monroe doll poses for her eBay portrait in Joanna Schmergel's home (click to enlarge).

readers from Lincoln with pairs of students—offered to sell the dolls on eBay to raise money for the MCC. After researching each doll's history and value, she posed them artfully in various spots in her house to photograph them.

Rosen's mother collected the dolls over about 20 years. Most are from the Franklin Mint, although there are also some older antique dolls and random doll-related or doll-house-related items. "I bought her a doll once for her birthday, and that's what caused her to have an interest in them," he said. "She always loved her dollhouse as a little girl, so I think somehow this struck a nerve and she enjoyed it."

(continued)

The items are listed on Schmergel's eBay store. As of September 9, 20 dolls had been sold for a total $998.91 and shipped to buyers in seven states as well as France, Poland and Great Britain, she reported. She hopes to clear $3,000 if the other 40 dolls still on the site are sold.

In addition to Rosen's dolls, Schmergel is seeking donations of American Girl dolls in good condition for her eBay auction, because they have a a high resale value and are less costly to package than porcelain.

The MCC's annual budget has grown from about $9,000 in 2014-15 to $13,000 in 2016-17, according to MCC liaison Pilar Doughty. This summer, the MCC collaborated with the METCO office, the Parks and Recreation Department, and the Codman Trust to provide almost full scholarships to Lincoln Summer Day Camp for 29 Boston-based children. During the school year, the MCC also helps pay for bus transportation for METCO kids who want to participate in the Lincoln After-school Activities Program (LEAP).

In addition, the organization partnered last year with the Lincoln Land Conservation Trust, Stonegate Gardens and the PTO to get kids involved in community activities such as fall bulb-planting in Lincoln's pollinator meadow and a day of scarecrow-making in October.

The MCC's biggest non-monetary need is volunteers to help run programs and chaperone events. "Without committed volunteers who can take a leadership role, we can't continue to offer the diverse programs and social engagement opportunities that we were able to offer last year," Doughty said.

Later this year, the MCC—which is now a registered nonprofit that can accept tax-deductible donations—hopes to hold a fund-raising event. And the dolls definitely help.

"Much as I would love to take credit for any of this, the reality is that it was 100% Joanna's effort, ideas, and energy that caused this to happen," Rosen said. "I was simply looking to part with these dolls, and she turned it into an awesome opportunity to do something helpful and kind for our extended community."

The Lincoln Squirrel (www.lincolnsquirrel.com) is Lincoln's news website. To read the article online, go to **tinyurl.com/squirrel-17.**

Sales of dolls, antiques providing big share of MCC budget

October 10, 2018 by Alice Waugh (Edit)

What began last year as an eBay auction of donated vintage dolls has turned into a multipronged nonprofit effort that has netted thousands of dollars for METCO and provided summer camp scholarships for 34 kids.

Joanne Schmergel's Cerulean Way home is slowly being taken over by dolls, antiques and other items she's collecting and selling to benefit the METCO Coordinating Committee. What was once an office become, in her words, "a full-blown doll shop, and our formal dining room is a living estate sale."

Joanna Schmergel (left) and Erica Gonella, MCC treasurer and director of annual giving, in a room full of dolls to be sold by the organization (click images to enlarge).

When the MCC first began supporting the summer camp program, they dedicated a majority of funds from its annual mailing campaign—but this drastically reduced the funds available during the school year to pay for late METCO buses, MCC president Pilar Doughty said. When Schmergel approached the group with her doll sales idea, "we thought 'we don't have anything to lose.' Little did we imagine that she'd be able to raise enough money to make doll sales the new cornerstone of our Boston-based student summer camp funding in 2017-18."

(continued)

A donated painting for sale, which Schmergel jokingly titles "Why Did We Buy a Farm Share?"

Last year, doll sales netted $7,800, or 45 percent of the MCC's total annual budget. This allowed the group offer full scholarships to 48 Boston-based, METCO-enrolled Lincoln School children to the four-week Lincoln Parks & Recreation summer camp, allowing them to attend at minimal cost to them (though only 34 kids wound up participating).

Schmergel, who is in charge of MCC's fundraising and special projects, collected more donated inventory during the summer, including 30 American Girl dolls (now on sale in individual baskets for $59.99 each) and 200 collectible Barbie dolls donated by Lincoln resident Erica Mason that will likely net $3,500–$4,500 on eBay. The MCC also plans to sell antique and vintage dolls at the Boston Toy Show and is marketing more items on LincolnTalk, including four Chinese mud clay figures and various estate-sale items.

The next goal is raising money through various methods fund Boston-based middle-schoolers who would like to attend Lincoln Summer Day Camp. Because the middle camp tuition is costlier and the transportation logistics are tricky, the MCC hasn't been able to advertise the camp scholarship program widely to middle schoolers.

Chinese figurines for sale by the MCC.

"The MCC had seen steady, gradual decline in both volunteerism and monetary donations over the past five years, and this seriously impacted the number and frequency of programs that we have been able to offer," Doughty said. "When Joanna came to the team with renewed energy and a 'can-do and will-do' attitude, she provided a breath of fresh air. Knowing that we're on stable financial ground for the year (because of her fundraiser) allows our leadership team to step out of panic mode and plan more effectively for the future."

To read this article online, go to **tinyurl.com/squirrel-18.**

6 MINUTE READ

ALUMNI PROFILE

from **Norwich Record** | **Winter 2021**
by **Norwich University**

SERVICE CHANGING LIVES, ONE ANTIQUE AT A TIME

How Joanna Owen Schmergel '99 put her MBA and Airborne training to use to help Boston-area students

BY JANE DUNBAR

The Lincoln, Mass., METCO Coordinating Committee (MCC) was established in 1966 with a mission to strengthen diversity within the suburban town's public schools, initially by organizing transportation for students of color from Boston neighborhoods. MCC had always enjoyed broad community endorsement. But as the pool of mostly older donors narrowed and the list of volunteers shortened in more recent years, the committee struggled to keep pace with its expanding wish list of initiatives they hoped to support.

That's when Joanna Owen Schmergel '99 parachuted onto the scene.

A former lieutenant in the Army's elite 82nd Airborne Division, Joanna had moved to the predominantly white suburb in 2013 with her husband and toddler with a second child on the way. One morning six years ago, she opened her inbox to an appeal from Erica Gonella, MCC treasurer.

NORWICH UNIVERSITY CONNECTIONS

Photograph by Jason Grow

(continued)

The Norwich Bulletin, a magazine produced by Norwich University (Joanna's alma mater), published this story about her MCC work in its winter 2021 issue. To read this article online, go to **tinyurl.com/schmergel.**

"It really touched me," Schmergel recalls. "I hadn't heard of the organization, but its mission of diversity, equity, and inclusion is something my late father had always been very passionate about. So I impulsively made a gift in his honor."

It was a fairly significant gift, one noticed by the MCC president at the time, Pilar Doughty.

"Out of nowhere we get this donation from Joanna, see that she has a young family, and realized that we had to reach out," Doughty said. Schmergel responded by jumping feet-first, Airborne style, into the opportunity to carry her father's legacy forward.

From the get-go, she brought the same motivation and doggedness to her new volunteer venture that had characterized her time on the Hill. (While at Norwich, Schmergel was one of only two Norwich cadets to earn the double tab reserved for graduates of both Air Assault School and Airborne School.) She also brought the business acumen she'd acquired from her MBA program at Simmons College in Boston.

In six short years, Schmergel has helped guide the process of organizing the MCC as a 501(c)(3) entity; has participated in MCC's school-based reading program to address literacy and achievement gaps among kindergartners; and established an MCC-funded scholarship program so that Lincoln's Boston-resident students can attend the town's annual four-week summer day camp. Most notably, Schmergel also established a running estate sale called "Downsize for Diversity" that engages a dozen volunteers who inspire hundreds of donors and buyers from countless communities around the state to support MCC's mission and programming. Since 2017, the enterprise has raised nearly $100,000 toward an endowment fund that will help ensure MCC's impact well into the future. A portion of those funds will also help facilitate a new racial justice and implicit bias training program in the Lincoln school system that ultimately will be open to the entire community.

Doughty, who has since moved on from her role as MCC president to serve on its board and as co-chair of the Lincoln PTO, credits Schmergel's military background for her outsized impact on METCO HISTORY The Metropolitan Council for Educational Opportunity (METCO) is a Massachusetts program established in 1966 to increase diversity and reduce racial isolation in the public school system. Initially funded by a grant from the Carnegie Foundation and the United States Department of Education, METCO matches students within the Boston and Springfield school districts with participating suburban host communities. It remains the largest, and second oldest, voluntary program of its kind in the country. Today, nearly 3,300 Boston-based students attend school in one of 38 different districts outside the city, including Lincoln.

the organization. An Air Force veteran herself, she recognizes in Schmergel the authority, attention to detail, and ability to take care of others that characterize a true leader.

"She pitches in at every level," Doughty says, "and she treats everyone who helps her with a tremendous amount of respect."

"My dad taught me that racial equality begins with children and how they're raised," Schmergel says. "I'm just honored to be part of a program that's helping ensure not only that my own children, but kids all over Lincoln, are growing up to be open-minded."

No doubt, her father would be proud.

Lincoln METCO committee downsizes for diversity; building relationships is the goal

Holly Camero Wicked Local

Published 6:39 a.m. ET Aug. 25, 2021 | Updated 1:16 p.m. ET Aug. 25, 2021

Building relationships is what drives the METCO Coordinating Committee, and four years ago they started a fundraiser – Downsize for Diversity – to help them do just that.

The concept is simple enough. Committee members solicit unwanted estate items and resell it.

However, the work involved is not quite so simple.

Metropolitan Council for Educational Opportunity *Courtesy Photo*

For Joanna Schmergel, who has been with the committee since 2015 and started the fundraiser in 2017, it is a full time job. Equipped with only a pickup truck and a few volunteers she picks up estate items, cleans and polishes them, measures and photographs the items, and even occasionally sands them down and stains them. She uses her house as a staging area, where people can purchase the items.

So far, the committee has raised about $122,000 and counting through Downsize for Diversity.

Building lasting relationships

Four years ago, the committee was struggling to get volunteers and raise enough money to pay expenses throughout the school year. Through the success of their fundraising efforts, in 2019 they realized they could raise enough money to start a policy governed fund that could help pay for programs throughout the school year and into perpetuity, Schmergel said.

Rebecca Blanchfield, committee treasurer, has put the funds in an investment account, where they continue to grow.

The money is used to help cement relationships between Lincoln students and students from Boston who attend Lincoln schools as part of the METCO program. The committee supports students in kindergarten to eighth grade.

"One of the core tenets of our mission is to build lasting relationships. We hope those relationships are lasting as all of those students go to the high school together," said Kristen Ferris, committee president.

(continued)

The committee subsidizes tuition for summer camp offered by Lincoln's Park and Recreation Department, so Boston students can attend. They also pay for buses to take Boston students home after attending after school programs, town events or playing sports.

"The idea being those relationships that you can develop at summer camp and you are playing together -- it extends that relationship building in important ways," said Ferris.

A COVID kind of year

Not surprisingly, COVID-19 upended METCO programming in 2020, but the committee rallied and found opportunities for Lincoln and Boston students to connect.

The committee partnered with Outschool, an organization that runs virtual enrichment and academic programs. They funded a virtual dance class and other programs, to provide some "outside of school time," added Ferris.

This year, they are hoping students can get together in person.

COVID has also impacted the committee's fundraising efforts, and with rising COVID cases throughout Middlesex County, the committee has once again shuttered the operation.

"This is our third COVID shutdown," said Schmergel. "When we feel it's not safe we shut down."

When they do restart, shoppers will be required to wear masks and socially distance.

Planning for the future

The group has started to come up with some fundraising ideas that would be less labor intensive. One of the ideas is to focus on art because it would be easier to move, said Blanchfield.

Halting the fundraising gives committee members more time to collaborate on the book they are writing – a blueprint of sorts – to share what they've learned from Downsize for Diversity.

"There's a tremendous number of baby boomers downsizing in Massachusetts and their children don't want their things. We want to share our story on exactly how to duplicate some of what we've done," said Schmergel.

The book will not be for profit, but rather given away or sold at cost.

"This is too much work to just benefit Lincoln METCO. We want it to benefit all the Friends of METCO in Massachusetts," said Schmergel.

Schmergel credits friends, neighbors, committee members, volunteers and 234 donors across 35 towns for the success of Downsize for Diversity.

"The village is powerful and we were able to do this and every other town that has a METCO program can do this too. When the community comes together and puts aside their differences we can do anything," she said.

For information about the METCO Coordinating Committee visit lincolnmcc.org/.

(continued)

More about METCO

The Metropolitan Council for Educational Opportunity is a voluntary program funded by the state of Massachusetts. Its goal is to expand educational opportunities and reduce racial, ethnic, and socioeconomic isolation by having students in Boston and Springfield attend public schools in participating communities.

Lincoln has participated in the METCO program since its start in 1966 and has the highest percentage of Boston students in the 33 participating suburban districts.

Today more than 90 children from various Boston neighborhoods are enrolled in kindergarten through eighth grade at the Lincoln Public Schools.

For information visit metcoinc.org/.

JOANNA OWEN SCHMERGEL

Throughout his life, Wadsworth "Waddy" Owen was committed to antiracism. As a nine year old in 1940's Jacksonville, Florida, he witnessed a car crash between Black and white families. He would never forget watching as an ambulance came to get the white family, and left the injured Black family alone on the side of the road. "It was the only time I ever saw him cry, when he told me that story," recalls his daughter Joanna Schmergel, who has followed in her late father's footsteps in Lincoln, Massachusetts.

As Fundraising Lead for **Lincoln's METCO Coordinating Committee** (MCC), Joanna has volunteered since 2017, raising a total of $84,581 for METCO student camp scholarships and late buses. Lincoln's MCC was founded in 1966, and has operated continuously by volunteer parents deeply committed to the program's success.

For Joanna, it all started with American Girl dolls, which were donated, refurbished, and resold to great success. That enterprise evolved into a full-scale online estate sale endeavor, all to support METCO students who attend school in Lincoln. Today Joanna obtains and resells antique furniture, artwork, and anything of value from private donors living in over 40 towns. "I've become a bit of an expert in pricing valuable items, and when I don't know, I have a community of support that jumps in to help," Joanna says.

With her focus on the estate sales, Joanna has now passed the American Girl doll project on to Lincoln's METCO Director **Marika Hamilton.** Marika has added a social entrepreneurship component: through reselling the dolls, students develop skills in marketing, sales, home economics, and philanthropy.

From the 2020-2021 METCO Annual Report.

Thank you to so many!

A huge thank-you to all 252 donors in all 33 donor towns (including Lincoln, which accounted for 48% of our donors):

Arlington	Carlisle	Lincoln	Sudbury
Auburndale	Chestnut Hill	Melrose	Wakefield
Bedford	Concord	Natick	Waltham
Belmont	Essex	Newton	Watertown
Bolton	Framingham	Plymouth	Wayland
Boston	Hudson	Reading	Wellesley
Brookline	Jamaica Plain	Roslindale	Weston
Cambridge	Lexington	Sherborn	Westford

Franklin Mint limited-edition Michelle Obama doll in inauguration gown (sold for $500 at Lincoln PTO picnic).

The Lincoln METCO Coordinating Committee
"It takes a village" never rang so true!

Rebecca Blanchfield

"Life's most urgent question is: What are you doing for others?"

— Martin Luther King Jr.

Hope White

"You have brains in your head. You have feet in your shoes. You can steer yourself in any direction you choose."

— Dr. Seuss

Becky Bermont

"Could a greater miracle take place than for us to look through each other's eyes for an instant?"

— Henry David Thoreau

Michelle Barnes and Erica Gonella

"The beauty of anti-racism is that you don't have to pretend to be free of racism to be an anti-racist. Anti-racism is the commitment to fight racism wherever you find it, including in yourself. And it's the only way forward."

— Ijeoma Oluo

Heather Ring

"Never be limited by other people's limited imaginations."

— Mae Jamison

Moha Desai

"When you see something that is not right, not fair, not just, say something, do something. Get in trouble, good trouble, necessary trouble."
— U.S. Rep. John Lewis

Pilar Doughty

"Love recognizes no barriers. It jumps hurdles, leaps fences, penetrates walls to arrive at its destination full of hope."
— Maya Angelou

Gina Halsted

"Don't ever underestimate the difference you can make because history has shown us that courage can be contagious and hope can take on a life of its own."
— Michelle Obama

Abigail Adams

"Got a cast-iron stove? No problem — we can move it! Anything to raise funds for MCC to support METCO!"

Hans Bitter and Dan Pereira

"Our ability to reach unity in diversity will be the beauty and the test of our civilization."

— Mahatma Ghandi

Rob Stringer

"Change is brought about because ordinary people do extraordinary things."
— Barack Obama

Jena Salon

"In our work and in our living, we must recognize that difference is a reason for celebration and growth, rather than a reason for destruction."
— Audre Lorde

Devon Burroughs

"The wrong question will always lead to the wrong answer.."
— Rev. Dr. Brenda Salter McNeil

Desmond Crowley

"The world is full of magic things, patiently waiting for our senses to grow sharper."
— William Butler Yeats

Jessica Packineau

"The greatness of a community is most accurately measured by the compassionate actions of its members,"
— Coretta Scott King

Heather Veague

"For there is always light. If only we're brave enough to see it. If only we're brave enough to be it."
— Amanda Gorman

Sarah Collmer
Principal, gradesK-4

"The significance of oneself cannot be measured by the fame and glory of this world or the material things we have, but by the love and compassion you have shown to others every day of your life, without fame or glory or thanks just in the name of love."
— *Mi Sun Ellis*

Sharon Hobbs
Principal, grades 5-8

"Do the best you can until you know better. Then when you know better, do better."
— *Maya Angelou*

Marika Hamilton

"Never doubt that a small group of thoughtful committed citizens can change the world: Indeed it's the only thing that ever has."
— *Margaret Mead*

"Injustice anywhere is a threat to justice everywhere."
— *Martin Luther King, Jr.*

Joanna Schmergel

Photo by Jason Grow

"America, we know, is composed of diverse communities. We have different languages, different skills, different talents and different religion. But when our way of life is threatened, like the freedom and liberty that we all cherish, we come together as one. And when we come together as one, we are invincible. We cannot be defeated."

— *Peter MacDonald Sr., one of eight surviving WWII Navajo code talkers, U.S. Marine Corps*

Anna Lucchese

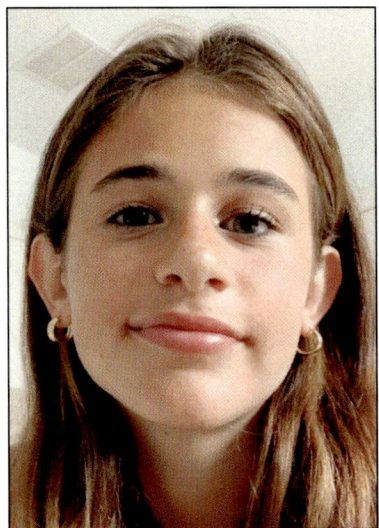

Anna is an eighth-grader at the Lincoln School in 2021-22. She designed the Downsize for Diversity logo seen on the cover of this book.

"I have always been a strong believer in equal rights and diversity, so being able to work on this project with the METCO program has been an amazing opportunity. I hope that my work helps others choose to help in making their community more diverse."

Josiah Jing Ren Chow

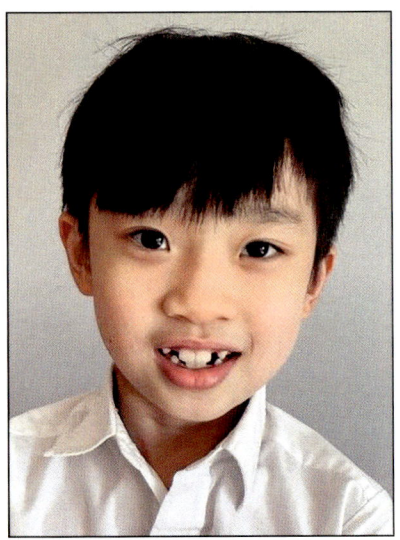

Josiah is a second-grader at the Lincoln School in 2021-22. He drew the pictures on the front and back cover.

"Diversity matters to me because it makes everybody special."

Aleco Buendia

Aleco helped convert hundreds of cellphone photos for use in print. He's a member of the Lincoln-Sudbury class of 2023.

"If we cannot do great things, we can do small things in a great way."

— Melnea Cass

Alice Waugh

Alice designed and edited this book based on Joanna's collection of photos and anecdotes. She is the editor of the Lincoln Squirrel, the town's news website.

"We are all different, which is great because we are all unique. Without diversity, life would be very boring."

— Catherine Pulsifer

"Hope is being able to see that there is light despite all of the darkness."

— *Desmond Tutu*

...And a *huge* thank-you from Joanna to her husband, Greg Schmergel, for helping her load and unload heavy furniture hundreds of times during the last four years and for being OK with this project taking over the family's house. And for modeling all those antique Japanese kimonos!

Greg Schmergel is a talented mimic of emu expressions (Greg is on the left).

109

Our most invaluable helper, Big Bertha

Big Bertha is a 2012 Dodge Ram 1500 pickup truck purchased by the Schmergel family in 2015. In addition to all the work she does for Lincoln METCO, she also pulls the trailer with a live rock band in the Lincoln Fourth of July parade each year while also serving as the Lincoln METCO parade float.

Above: Aline Ribeiro (an au pair for the Schmergels from São Paulo, Brazil) takes center stage on the Fourth of July as Lady Liberty.

Left to right: The Nays (in loud shirts), a band of Lincoln School alums who play at Lincoln's July 4 celebration every year, various MCC members, and au pair Aline Ribeiro (in green).

111